INTRODUCING
ISSUES WITH
OPPOSING
VIEWPOINTS®

Alcohol

Lauri S. Friedman, *Book Editor*

I.C.C. LIBRARY

GREENHAVEN PRESS
A part of Gale, Cengage Learning

GALE
CENGAGE Learning™

Detroit • New York • San Francisco • New Haven, Conn • Waterville, Maine • London

GALE
CENGAGE Learning™

Christine Nasso, *Publisher*
Elizabeth Des Chenes, *Managing Editor*

© 2010 Greenhaven Press, a part of Gale, Cengage Learning

Gale and Greenhaven Press are registered trademarks used herein under license.

For more information, contact:
Greenhaven Press
27500 Drake Rd.
Farmington Hills, MI 48331-3535
Or you can visit our Internet site at gale.cengage.com

Articles in Greenhaven Press anthologies are often edited for length to meet page requirements. In addition, original titles of these works are changed to clearly present the main thesis and to explicitly indicate the author's opinion. Every effort is made to ensure that Greenhaven Press accurately reflects the original intent of the authors. Every effort has been made to trace the owners of copyrighted material.

Cover image © Ilene MacDonald/Alamy.

LIBRARY OF CONGRESS CATALOGING-IN-PUBLICATION DATA

Alcohol / Lauri S. Friedman, book editor.
    p. cm. -- (Introducing issues with opposing viewpoints)
  Includes bibliographical references and index.
  ISBN 978-0-7377-4730-0 (hbk.)
  1. Drinking of alcoholic beverages--United States--Juvenile literature. 2. Binge drinking--United States--Juvenile literature. 3. Youth--Alcohol use--United States--Juvenile literature. I. Friedman, Lauri S.
  HV5292.A3792 2010
  362.2920973--dc22
                        2009050773

Printed in the United States of America
1 2 3 4 5 6 7 14 13 12 11 10

Contents

Foreword

Indulging in a wide spectrum of ideas, beliefs, and perspectives is a critical cornerstone of democracy. After all, it is often debates over differences of opinion, such as whether to legalize abortion, how to treat prisoners, or when to enact the death penalty, that shape our society and drive it forward. Such diversity of thought is frequently regarded as the hallmark of a healthy and civilized culture. As the Reverend Clifford Schutjer of the First Congregational Church in Mansfield, Ohio, declared in a 2001 sermon, "Surrounding oneself with only like-minded people, restricting what we listen to or read only to what we find agreeable is irresponsible. Refusing to entertain doubts once we make up our minds is a subtle but deadly form of arrogance." With this advice in mind, Introducing Issues with Opposing Viewpoints books aim to open readers' minds to the critically divergent views that comprise our world's most important debates.

Introducing Issues with Opposing Viewpoints simplifies for students the enormous and often overwhelming mass of material now available via print and electronic media. Collected in every volume is an array of opinions that captures the essence of a particular controversy or topic. Introducing Issues with Opposing Viewpoints books embody the spirit of nineteenth-century journalist Charles A. Dana's axiom: "Fight for your opinions, but do not believe that they contain the whole truth, or the only truth." Absorbing such contrasting opinions teaches students to analyze the strength of an argument and compare it to its opposition. From this process readers can inform and strengthen their own opinions, or be exposed to new information that will change their minds. Introducing Issues with Opposing Viewpoints is a mosaic of different voices. The authors are statesmen, pundits, academics, journalists, corporations, and ordinary people who have felt compelled to share their experiences and ideas in a public forum. Their words have been collected from newspapers, journals, books, speeches, interviews, and the Internet, the fastest growing body of opinionated material in the world.

Introducing Issues with Opposing Viewpoints shares many of the well-known features of its critically acclaimed parent series, Opposing Viewpoints. The articles are presented in a pro/con format, allowing readers to absorb divergent perspectives side by side. Active reading questions preface each viewpoint, requiring the student to approach the material thoughtfully and carefully. Useful charts, graphs, and cartoons supplement each article. A thorough introduction provides readers with crucial background on an issue. An annotated bibliography points the reader toward articles, books, and Web sites that contain additional information on the topic. An appendix of organizations to contact contains a wide variety of charities, nonprofit organizations, political groups, and private enterprises that each hold a position on the issue at hand. Finally, a comprehensive index allows readers to locate content quickly and efficiently.

Introducing Issues with Opposing Viewpoints is also significantly different from Opposing Viewpoints. As the series title implies, its presentation will help introduce students to the concept of opposing viewpoints and learn to use this material to aid in critical writing and debate. The series' four-color, accessible format makes the books attractive and inviting to readers of all levels. In addition, each viewpoint has been carefully edited to maximize a reader's understanding of the content. Short but thorough viewpoints capture the essence of an argument. A substantial, thought-provoking essay question placed at the end of each viewpoint asks the student to further investigate the issues raised in the viewpoint, compare and contrast two authors' arguments, or consider how one might go about forming an opinion on the topic at hand. Each viewpoint contains sidebars that include at-a-glance information and handy statistics. A Facts About section located in the back of the book further supplies students with relevant facts and figures.

Following in the tradition of the Opposing Viewpoints series, Greenhaven Press continues to provide readers with invaluable exposure to the controversial issues that shape our world. As John Stuart Mill once wrote: "The only way in which a human being can make some approach to knowing the whole of a subject is by hearing what can be said about it by persons of every variety of opinion and studying all modes in which it can be looked at by every character of mind. No wise man ever acquired his wisdom in any mode but this." It is to this principle that Introducing Issues with Opposing Viewpoints books are dedicated.

Introduction

While alcohol has been around for thousands of years, binge drinking (drinking five or more drinks at a time) among America's youth is a relatively new problem, one that has become so serious, some call it an epidemic. Ironically, binge drinking is most severe in places renowned for learning and intellectual development: America's college and university campuses. According to the American Medical Association, binge drinking is responsible for 1,400 deaths, 500,000 injuries, and 70,000 sexual assaults on campuses each year. How to best reduce binge drinking is therefore a hotly debated topic among the nation's health officials, policy makers, and, increasingly, its college presidents.

In 2008 a group of college presidents came together to form the Amethyst Initiative, which called for the minimum drinking age to be lowered to eighteen. The idea behind this movement was that lowering the drinking age would help young people form a responsible relationship with alcohol earlier in life, the way they do in places like Europe, where most countries have a drinking age of eighteen or even sixteen. In these environments, young people are more likely to respect alcohol and enjoy it maturely and in moderation. Because it is not forbidden to them, alcohol seems less alluring and is thus less likely to be abused. Young Europeans are more likely to have a "what's the big deal" attitude toward alcohol, and are much less likely to binge drink when they are on their own for the first time. In contrast, because alcohol is denied to American students, they overindulge in it the first chance they get when they are away from home.

Those who support the Amethyst Initiative argue that young people are going to drink, and so it is better to help them become familiar and comfortable with alcohol earlier so they do not abuse it later on. Says John M. McCardell Jr., president of Middlebury College: "Alcohol is a reality in the lives of young adults. We can either try to change the reality—which has been our principal focus since 1984, by imposing prohibition on young adults 18 to 20—or we can create the safest possible environment for the reality."[1] In his opinion, the minimum legal drinking age of twenty-one has not changed young peoples' desire to drink, and so it is time to try something different.

How Many Drinks Are Too Many?

Men and women have different tolerances for alcohol, but everyone has had too much to drink and drive after just a couple of drinks. The legal blood-alcohol content (BAC) limit to drive is .08, but most motorists' skills are impaired before they reach that point.

Men — Approximate Blood-Alcohol Percentage

Drinks	Body Weight in Pounds								Result
	100	120	140	160	180	200	220	240	
0	.00	.00	.00	.00	.00	.00	.00	.00	Only safe driving limit
1	.04	.03	.03	.02	.02	.02	.02	.02	Driving skills significantly affected
2	.08	.06	.05	.05	.04	.04	.03	.03	Driving skills significantly affected
3	.11	.09	.08	.07	.06	.06	.05	.05	Driving skills significantly affected
4	.15	.12	.11	.09	.08	.08	.07	.06	Possible criminal penalties
5	.19	.16	.13	.12	.11	.09	.09	.08	Possible criminal penalties
6	.23	.19	.16	.14	.13	.11	.10	.09	Legally intoxicated
7	.26	.22	.19	.16	.15	.13	.12	.11	Legally intoxicated
8	.30	.25	.21	.19	.17	.15	.14	.13	Criminal penalties
9	.34	.28	.24	.21	.19	.17	.15	.14	Criminal penalties
10	.38	.31	.27	.23	.21	.19	.17	.16	Death possible

Women — Approximate Blood-Alcohol Percentage

Drinks	Body Weight in Pounds									Result
	90	100	120	140	160	180	200	220	240	
0	.00	.00	.00	.00	.00	.00	.00	.00	.00	Only safe driving limit
1	.05	.05	.04	.03	.03	.03	.02	.02	.02	Driving skills significantly affected
2	.10	.09	.08	.07	.06	.05	.05	.04	.04	Driving skills significantly affected
3	.15	.14	.11	.10	.09	.08	.07	.06	.06	Driving skills significantly affected
4	.20	.18	.15	.13	.11	.10	.09	.08	.08	Possible criminal penalties
5	.25	.23	.19	.16	.14	.13	.11	.10	.09	Possible criminal penalties
6	.30	.27	.23	.19	.17	.15	.14	.12	.11	Legally intoxicated
7	.35	.32	.27	.23	.20	.18	.16	.14	.13	Legally intoxicated
8	.40	.36	.30	.26	.23	.20	.18	.17	.15	Criminal penalties
9	.45	.41	.34	.29	.26	.23	.20	.19	.17	Criminal penalties
10	.51	.45	.38	.32	.28	.25	.23	.21	.19	Death possible

Subtract .01 percent for each 40 minutes of drinking. One drink is 1.25 oz. of 80 proof liquor, 12 oz. of beer, or 5 oz. of table wine.

Taken from: Be Responsible About Drinking (BRAD), 2008. www.brad21.org.

McCardell is one of 135 college presidents who, to date, have signed the Amethyst Initiative because they believe that lowering the drinking age will encourage responsible drinking habits among America's youth.

But others are incredulous at the suggestion to lower the drinking age. In their minds, the solution to irresponsible drinking among young people is not to let them have alcohol even earlier. They point to data from the 1960s and 1970s, when most states had a legal drinking age of eighteen or nineteen. During this time, rates of alcohol-related traffic fatalities skyrocketed, as did rates of alcohol-related violence and murder among eighteen- to twenty-year-olds. "It's not rocket science to figure out what would happen if the college presidents have their way with the drinking age," says sociology professor Robert Nash Parker. "Hundreds more dead young people each year. Sexual assaults, alcohol-related fights and other injuries would also increase."[2] Parker and others believe the college presidents who support a lowered drinking age are not thinking clearly about the many problems solved by the higher drinking age.

Other studies have shown that binge drinking seems to be exclusively a problem on college campuses, which makes people even less supportive of lowering the drinking age. In fact, a twenty-seven-year study by the National Survey on Drug Use and Health found that binge drinking by men between eighteen and twenty years old who did *not* attend college dropped by more than 30 percent during that period. This would indicate that eighteen- to twenty-year-olds who do not go to college do not wrestle with binge drinking in the way that college students do—and so the problem is not with the drinking age but with the college environment. It could be that college campuses promote binge drinking by hosting fraternities and sororities or by allowing a peer-pressure environment that encourages binge drinking. In this case, it appears that the solution to binge drinking lies more with college regulations than with the national minimum drinking age.

Outreach and intervention programs are looked to as another way to reduce the binge drinking problem among the nation's students. Such programs focus on helping teens understand the risks and consequences of binge drinking—and some have met with great success. For example, a 2009 study published in the *Archives of Pediatrics and Adolescent Medicine* concluded that prevention programs can reduce binge drinking rates among young people by as much as one-third. One such program, called Communities That Care, was found to have this effect on eighth-grade students. The rates of binge drinking among students who went through the program were 37 percent lower than those who did not. Said J. David Hawkins, a founder of the program, "We know kids who drink that way are at risk for developing alcohol abuse and dependence later. This binge drinking is occurring when children are 13 and 14 years of age, so we are actually preventing the likelihood of later alcohol problems. This is very important from a public health standpoint."[3] School and health officials are hopeful that exposing more young people to prevention programs can further reduce binge drinking rates over time.

Whether prevention programs or lowering the drinking age is the key to reducing binge drinking is as yet unclear—but everyone can agree that binge drinking among the nation's students constitutes a serious problem. How to best reduce binge drinking is just one of the many arguments presented in *Introducing Issues with Opposing Viewpoints: Alcohol.* Pro/con article pairs expose readers to the basic debates surrounding alcohol and encourage them to develop their own opinions on the topic.

Notes

1. John M. McCardell Jr., "Drinking Age of 21 Doesn't Work," CNN .com, September 16, 2009. www.cnn.com/2009/POLITICS/09/16/ mccardell.lower.drinking.age/index.html.

2. Robert Nash Parker, "Too Young to Drink," *Los Angeles Times,* August 27, 2008. http://articles.latimes.com/2008/aug/27/news/ OE-PARKER27.

3. Quoted in Joel Schwarz, "Rate of Teen Binge Drinking Cut More Than One-Third by Prevention System," *University of Washington News,* September 7, 2009. http://uwnews.org/article .asp?articleID=51818.

Chapter 1

Does Alcohol Pose a Threat to Society?

The extent to which underage drinking threatens society is unclear and hotly debated.

Underage Drinking Is a Crisis That Threatens Society

"Underage alcohol use is a pervasive problem with serious health and safety consequences for the nation."

U.S. Department of Health and Human Services

In the following viewpoint the U.S. Department of Health and Human Services argues that underage drinking is a widespread crisis that threatens all of society. The authors say that kids start drinking as early as nine years old and, as they move through adolescence, will tend to binge drink. Such behavior puts them at risk for death by accident, injury, and suicide; disease, including sexually transmitted diseases (STDs); physical and sexual assault; unplanned pregnancy; brain damage; criminal activity; and other problems. As a result, the authors conclude that underage drinking is a pervasive problem that affects the entire country.

The U.S. Department of Health and Human Services is a branch of the government charged with protecting Americans' health and providing them with essential human services.

U.S. Department of Human Health and Human Services, *The Surgeon General's Call to Action to Prevent and Reduce Underage Drinking,* Washington, DC: U.S. Department of Human Health and Human Services, 2007. Reproduced by permission.

AS YOU READ, CONSIDER THE FOLLOWING QUESTIONS:
1. According to the authors, by age fifteen what percent of boys and girls have tried alcohol? What percent have tried it by age twenty-one?
2. What percent of nine- to ten-year-olds do the authors say have started drinking?
3. List at least five consequences the authors say result from underage drinking.

U nderage alcohol consumption in the United States is a widespread and persistent public health and safety problem that creates serious personal, social, and economic consequences for adolescents, their families, communities, and the nation as a whole. Alcohol is the drug of choice among America's adolescents, used by more young people than tobacco or illicit drugs. The prevention and reduction of underage drinking and treatment of underage youth with alcohol use disorders (AUDs) are therefore important public health and safety goals. . . .

The Problem Goes Beyond Drunk Driving

Although considerable attention has been focused on the serious consequences of underage drinking and driving, accumulating evidence indicates that the range of adverse consequences is much more extensive than that and should also be comprehensively addressed. For example, the highest prevalence of alcohol dependence in the U.S. population is among 18- to 20-year-olds who typically began drinking years earlier. This finding underscores the need to consider problem drinking within a developmental framework.

Furthermore, early and, especially, early heavy drinking are associated with increased risk for adverse lifetime alcohol-related consequences. Research also has provided a more complete understanding of how underage drinking is related to factors in the adolescent's environment, cultural issues, and an adolescent's individual characteristics. Taken together, these data demonstrate the compelling need to address alcohol problems early, continuously, and in the context of human development using a systematic approach that spans childhood through adolescence into adulthood.

In the United States, 50 percent of boys and girls aged fifteen have consumed alcohol.

A Serious and Ongoing Problem

Underage drinking remains a serious problem despite laws against it in all 50 States; decades of Federal, State, Tribal, and local programs aimed at preventing and reducing underage drinking; and efforts by many private entities. Underage drinking is deeply embedded in the American culture, is often viewed as a rite of passage, is frequently facilitated by adults, and has proved stubbornly resistant to change. A new, more comprehensive and developmentally sensitive approach is warranted. The growing body of research in the developmental area, including identification of risk and protective factors for underage alcohol use, supports the more complex prevention and reduction strategies. . . .

Underage alcohol use increases with age. Alcohol use is an age-related phenomenon. The percentage of the population who have drunk at least one whole drink rises steeply during adolescence until it plateaus at about age 21. By age 15, approximately 50 percent of boys and girls have had a whole drink of alcohol; by age 21, approximately 90 percent have done so.

There is a high prevalence of alcohol use disorders among the young. Early alcohol consumption by some young people will result in an alcohol use disorder—that is, they will meet diagnostic criteria for either alcohol abuse or dependence. The highest prevalence of alcohol dependence is among people ages 18–20. . . .

Even some youth younger than age 18 have an alcohol use disorder. According to data from the 2005 National Survey on Drug Use and Health (NSDUH), 5.5 percent of youth ages 12–17 meet the diagnostic criteria for alcohol abuse or dependence.

Teens Drink Early and Heavily

Underage alcohol use is a pervasive problem with serious health and safety consequences for the nation. The nature and gravity of the problem is best described in terms of the number of children and adolescents who drink, when and how they drink, and the negative consequences that result from drinking.

Alcohol is the most widely used substance of abuse among America's youth. A higher percentage of youth in 8th, 10th, and 12th grades used alcohol in the month prior to being surveyed than used tobacco or marijuana, the illicit drug most commonly used by adolescents.

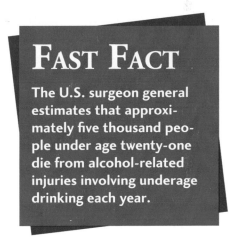

FAST FACT

The U.S. surgeon general estimates that approximately five thousand people under age twenty-one die from alcohol-related injuries involving underage drinking each year.

A substantial number of young people begin drinking at very young ages. A number of surveys ask youth about the age at which they first used alcohol. Because the methodology in the various surveys differs, the data are not consistent across them. Nonetheless, they do show that a substantial number of youth begin drinking before the age of 13. For example, data from recent surveys indicate that:

- Approximately 10 percent of 9- to 10-year-olds have started drinking.
- Nearly one-third of youth begin drinking before age 13.

- More than one-tenth of 12- or 13-year-olds and over one-third of 14- or 15-year-olds reported alcohol use (a whole drink) in the past year.
- The peak years of alcohol initiation are 7th and 8th grades.

Adolescents drink less frequently than adults, but when they do drink, they drink more heavily than adults. When youth between the ages of 12 and 20 consume alcohol, they drink on average about five drinks per occasion about six times a month. This amount of alcohol puts an adolescent drinker in the binge range, which, depending on the study, is defined as "five or more drinks on one occasion" or "five or more drinks in a row for men and four or more drinks in a row for women." By comparison, adult drinkers age 26 and older consume on average two to three drinks per occasion about nine times a month. . . .

The Consequences of Underage Drinking

The short- and long-term consequences that arise from underage alcohol consumption are astonishing in their range and magnitude, affecting adolescents, the people around them, and society as a whole. Adolescence is a time of life characterized by robust physical health and low incidence of disease, yet overall morbidity and mortality rates increase 200 percent between middle childhood and late adolescence/early adulthood. This dramatic rise is attributable in large part to the increase in risk-taking, sensation-seeking, and erratic behavior that follows the onset of puberty and which contributes to violence, unintentional injuries, risky sexual behavior, homicide, and suicide. Alcohol frequently plays a role in these adverse outcomes and the human tragedies they produce. Among the most prominent adverse consequences of underage alcohol use are those listed below. Underage drinking:

- Is a leading contributor to death from injuries, which are the main cause of death for people under age 21. Annually, about 5,000 people under age 21 die from alcohol-related injuries involving underage drinking. About 1,900 (38 percent) of the 5,000 deaths involve motor vehicle crashes, about 1,600 (32 percent) result from homicides, and about 300 (6 percent) result from suicides.

The Nature of Underage Drinking

Alcohol is the most widely abused substance among America's youth. More eighth, tenth, and twelfth graders used alcohol in the month prior to being surveyed than used tobacco or marijuana.

More Adolescents Use Alcohol than Use Cigarettes or Marijuana

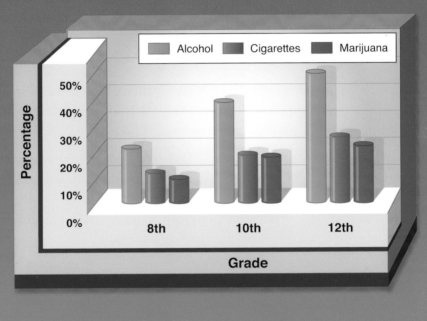

Taken from: Monitoring the Future Survey, 2006.

- Plays a significant role in risky sexual behavior, including unwanted, unintended, and unprotected sexual activity, and sex with multiple partners. Such behavior increases the risk for unplanned pregnancy and for contracting sexually transmitted diseases (STDs), including infection with HIV, the virus that causes AIDS.
- Increases the risk of physical and sexual assault.
- Is associated with academic failure.
- Is associated with illicit drug use.
- Is associated with tobacco use.

- Can cause a range of physical consequences, from hangovers to death from alcohol poisoning.
- Can cause alterations in the structure and function of the developing brain, which continues to mature into the mid- to late twenties, and may have consequences reaching far beyond adolescence.
- Creates secondhand effects that can put others at risk. Loud and unruly behavior, property destruction, unintentional injuries, violence, and even death because of underage alcohol use afflict innocent parties. For example, about 45 percent of people who die in crashes involving a drinking driver under the age of 21 are people other than the driver. Such secondhand effects often strike at random, making underage alcohol use truly everybody's problem.
- In conjunction with pregnancy, may result in fetal alcohol spectrum disorders, including fetal alcohol syndrome, which remains a leading cause of mental retardation.

Further, underage drinking is a risk factor for heavy drinking later in life, and continued heavy use of alcohol leads to increased risk across the lifespan for acute consequences and for medical problems such as cancers of the oral cavity, larynx, pharynx, and esophagus; liver cirrhosis; pancreatitis; and hemorrhagic stroke.

EVALUATING THE AUTHORS' ARGUMENTS:

This viewpoint was written by the Department of Health and Human Services, a branch of the U.S. government. Does the fact that this is a government source influence your opinion of it in any way? Are you more or less likely to agree with it than the next viewpoint, which was written by a journalist? Explain why or why not.

Viewpoint

2

Underage Drinking Is Not a Crisis

Suzy Dean

In the following viewpoint reporter Suzy Dean criticizes Scotland's efforts to curb underage drinking. She describes programs in which policemen stop young people on the street and test their sodas for alcohol, and punish parents if they give their kids any alcohol. Dean says police time would be better spent pursuing real criminals and believes the government has no right to clamp down on individual freedoms. In Dean's opinion, underage drinking is a harmless rite of passage, just a normal part of growing up. She also thinks that making it harder for teens to drink only makes them more curious about alcohol. What is best for everyone is to teach teens to drink responsibly, she concludes.

Suzy Dean is a writer, journalist, and co-organizer of the Manifesto Club, a group that campaigns against the extreme regulation of everyday life.

> *"It is hard to see how anybody can learn to drink responsibly if they are stopped from drinking."*

Suzy Dean, "War on Alcohol Threatens Individual Freedom," The Free Society, August 13, 2008.
Copyright © 2009 The Free Society.

With the summer holidays in full swing, the government's attention has predictably turned to teenage drinking. Following a 'successful' pilot in West Lothian [Scotland] where a ban on selling alcohol to under 21's at the weekends was implemented, the 'Changing Scotland's Relationship with Alcohol' consultation paper suggested that a blanket ban on selling any alcohol to under 21's become law across Scotland.

Moreover, it recommends that alcohol should be sold at a separate counter in supermarkets, like tobacco, to remind young people in particular that alcohol is different from other shopping products. As if they didn't know.

Far from trying to promote a continental style 'cafe culture' as planned when the introduction of late licensing laws for pubs and bars was introduced, it seems that the UK's [United Kingdom's] political elite would rather try to control who can drink, how much and where, particularly when it comes to teenage drinking.

Teach Young People *How* to Drink

It is hard to see how anybody can learn to drink responsibly if they are stopped from drinking. Policy is increasingly geared, naively, towards trying to discourage young people from drinking at all rather than encouraging police to deal with silly behaviour with discretion. The proposal to ban alcohol sales to under 21's in Scotland follows a number of earlier disproportionate measures.

In several Cambridgeshire communities, plain-clothed officers have been given the task of seizing alcohol from under 18's. And in Newcastle-Under-Lyme, police have been given powers to 'dip-stick test' young people's soft drinks for alcohol. Leaving aside the consideration that police should have better things to be getting on with, it seems odd that what has traditionally been a sort of rite of passage for teenagers is now being so heavily policed. These proposals and policies mistakenly assume that holding your drink comes with age rather than experience.

The need to protect people's health is an oft-cited argument for stopping young people from drinking. However, drinking policy seems vastly out of proportion to the impact that alcohol misuse has on individuals' health. Last month [July 2008] the NHS [National Health Service] Information Centre carried out a survey which revealed that not only is the rate of drug-taking, smoking and drinking amongst 11–15 year-olds falling, but the number of kids that have never tasted an alcoholic drink has risen from 39% in 2003 to 46% in 2007. Furthermore, yearly alcohol-related deaths stood at around 8,380 in 2004, a tiny number in proportion to [a] UK population of nearly 60 million.

It Is Not the Government's Business

The key reason for the authorities' concern over young people's alcohol intake is the tendency to link drinking to anti-social behaviour. As one sergeant policing under-18s' white lightning consumption in Cambridge commented, "We want to send a clear message that it is not acceptable for underage teens to be drinking and causing disorder in public areas".

Similarly, in Newcastle-under-Lyme a local councillor commented that the council hopes the dipping tests on teenagers' drinks will lead to a 'trouble free summer'. The idea of alcohol leading to anti-social rather than a pro-social behaviour is assumed without contention as the government increasingly regulates public space, demonising those young people that choose to drink, regardless of their behaviour.

> **FAST FACT**
>
> According to the New Mexico departments of Health and Public Education, alcohol use among teens dropped from 50.7 percent in 2003 to 43.2 percent in 2007.

The focus on teenage drinking has not only problematised growing up but damaged the authority of adults. Moving on from simply

In Scotland, police can test teenagers' soft drinks for the presence of alcohol at any time.

branding parents feckless for letting their teenagers have a drink, the government have started to actively punish them. Cambridgeshire police have already given out five penalties to parents for 'supplying' their kids with alcohol, making children of parents (as well as of teenagers).

Indeed, recently, a ban on happy hours in pubs was recommended by an independent review that sought to investigate the link between 'price promotion and alcohol abuse'—the emphasis of course being on the inability of people, in this case adults, to control themselves while under the influence.

Underage Drinking Is Largely Harmless

The view that the public has an alcohol problem is primarily one held by the government, rather than the public at large. While teenagers spend their summer experimenting—a necessary part of growing up—and adults, as they always have done, respond as they see fit, the government increasingly enforces its version of the 'correct' way to deal with a largely harmless, and ultimately banal social phenomenon—drinking.

As with lecturing adults on how much they should drink, measures to stop young people drinking are going to be painfully ineffective—indeed possibly even more so, if accounts of today's reckless, amoral 'yoof' [youth] youngsters are to be believed. Anti-drinking measures are today a symbol of government impotence rather than a nation of hedonists. With no sense of who the public are or how to connect with them in any meaningful way, they try to manage the trivial, everyday decisions.

While government interference of this sort is not often rebuked (and is indeed welcomed, on occasion), it is important that we make a stand against what is the gradual criminalisation of an entire generation, which effectively denies young people the space and freedom to experiment—a major part of growing-up and becoming an independent adult.

EVALUATING THE AUTHORS' ARGUMENTS:

To make her argument, Dean casts underage drinking as a harmless rite of passage, a natural part of the experimentation that kids do as they grow up. What do you think? Is this how you would characterize underage drinking? After you state your opinion, write one or two sentences on what you think each of the other authors in this chapter would say about this claim.

Alcohol Bans Benefit Society

SafeBeaches.org

> *"Alcohol on crowded beaches creates major public safety problems."*

Alcohol bans benefit society, argues the organization SafeBeaches.org in the following viewpoint. The group argues that when alcohol is legal in places like beaches, the community experiences higher rates of fighting, crime, physical and sexual assault, vandalism, litter, and public unrest. Furthermore, those who drive to the beach and drink have to eventually drive home, and police will be able to catch only a fraction of all those drunk drivers. For the safety of the community, the organization argues that alcohol should be banned in public spaces like beaches.

SafeBeaches.org is a grassroots organization created out of concern that area beaches were becoming an unsafe playground for underage and binge drinking. In 2007 it played an important role in championing the passage of a law that outlawed alcohol on San Diego beaches.

AS YOU READ, CONSIDER THE FOLLOWING QUESTIONS:

1. List at least eight problems the author says are fueled by drinking on the beach.
2. What are two other states the author says have enacted alcohol beach bans?
3. How many police patrol hours does the author say were wasted handling alcohol-related problems at a San Diego beach during a 2007 riot?

We seek to have a safe, clean and fun beach environment we can enjoy.

We also want to be able to bring our families and guests to the beach to have an enjoyable time without being embarrassed, harassed or insulted.

For many years we have personally witnessed actions that would insult most of us if we were walking down the boardwalk or along the beach with our loved ones. Simply put, we are all San Diego citizens and we are tired of our beaches being overrun by inconsiderate people—many usually under the influence of alcohol.

The Problems Brought by Alcohol

These things are regular occurrences on a year round basis—not just limited to holidays or individual media reports.

- Minors drinking
- People fist fighting
- Constant shouting, yelling, bantering and badgering
- People exposing themselves
- People vomiting from too much drinking
- Hearing people cussing at each other
- Seeing couples groping each other
- Hear demeaning comments towards women
- Seeing all the variety of drinking game and other "toys" including, but not limited to, beer funnels, liquor luges, crazy bats, beer-pong tables and blow-up dolls
- Hearing amplified music from long distances

- Seeing trash and litter pile up—with trash cans in plain view
- Hearing chants and yelling from participants of various drinking games
- Having to deal with the large groups (i.e. 20–100 people) which essentially overtake large portions of the beach with no consideration for others (see all of above and magnify)
- Seeing people urinating or defecating around the neighborhoods with bathrooms within walking distance
- Seeing many of these people stagger from the beach drunk knowing a high percentage are getting in their vehicles and driving home—putting other drivers throughout the city at risk
- Seeing our Police officers, Life Guards, Fire and Rescue and Park Rangers taunted, harassed or threatened
- Having to explain to our children, who have witnessed many of the above actions and situations
- Hearing people blame any and all of the above problems (i.e. lack of bathrooms, not enough enforcement, not enough trash cans etc. etc.,) on the City, the Police or the neighbors of the beach communities; because they refuse to take personal responsibility for their own personal statements and actions or understanding the physical limits of our City government.
- Not being able to bring my family, my relatives, my friends, employees or out of town guests to the beach of *my* choice because some people are intent on doing some or all of the above without consideration for others.

We're tired of this behavior which is most often related to the excessive and outrageous drinking patterns of people visiting our beaches.

How many great community residents would never consider living at the beach or, have left the beach communities because they do not want to deal with the continual harassment?

Enough is enough. Let's take back our beaches so we can enjoy them together without a bunch of drunken yahoos ruining it for everyone. . . .

Alcohol Beach Bans Let Lifeguards Do Their Jobs

Beach communities from across the nation from Fort Lauderdale to Imperial Beach that have adopted alcohol free beach policies have seen

Alcohol Bans Reduce Crime

After a temporary alcohol ban took place on San Diego beaches in January 2008, alcohol-related disturbances and crimes plummeted. As a result, the city voted to make the alcohol ban permanent.

Detentions of Publicly Drunken Persons

Holiday	2007	2008	% Change
Memorial Day Weekend	24	10	-58%
July 4th Holiday Weekend	124	40	-67.7%
Labor Day Holiday	22	1	-95%

Beach Area Crimes

Crime	2007	2008	% Change
Murder	3	2	-33.3%
Rape	19	38	100%
Robbery	99	83	-16.2%
Aggravated Assault	225	201	-10.7%
Burglary	506	490	-3.2%
Larceny	1,933	1,726	-10.7%
Auto Theft	652	422	-35.3%

Taken from: The City of San Diego Report to the City Council, Report no. 08-154, October 15, 2008, pp. 6, 10. http://docs.sandiego.gov/reportstocouncil/2008/08-154.pdf.

rapid and dramatic decreases in crimes and alcohol related arrests. Under the trial ordinance San Diego will see the same decrease in alcohol related crimes.

If the trial ordinance is enacted, lifeguards, some of whom were forced to abandon their towers to deal with the Labor Day riot,[1] will be able to concentrate their attentions on saving swimmers instead of being forced to divert their attentions to out of control drunks on the sand.

1. On Labor Day in 2007, police in riot gear were called to break up an alcohol-fueled beach riot at San Diego's Pacific Beach.

Communities in California, Florida, and Hawaii have adopted alcohol bans on beaches to curb alcohol-related crimes.

It is well documented that alcohol on crowded beaches creates major public safety problems. San Diego Police have made thousands of alcohol related arrests for everything from drunk driving to underage drinking every year at those beaches where out of control drinking is permitted.

Soaring alcohol related crime is why every major urban beach community in Southern California and most other parts of the nation including Florida and Hawaii have already adopted alcohol free beach policies. As a result, the problems we experience in San Diego are concentrated as people from across the nation intent on abusing alcohol at the beach descend onto our beaches, some of the few remaining beaches where uncontrolled drinking is still permitted. . . .

Preventing Drunk Driving

The problems associated with out of control drinking at our beaches hardly stop at the edge of the sand. The impacts of uncontrolled drinking at the beach and the strain it places on our already strained public safety resources impact each and every neighborhood in San Diego.

Almost three quarters of the people arrested for drunk driving in our beach communities were on their way out of the beach area into other San Diego neighborhoods when they were stopped. Since the police can only stop a small fraction of drunk drivers, this means that beach drinking endangers the lives of San Diegans in neighborhoods far from the beach.

A Waste of Police Resources

For far too long our police department has been forced to assign a disproportionate number of officers to patrol the beaches to control unruly drunks. And even with that, another 20,000 police patrol hours were diverted from other neighborhoods to handle alcohol related problems at the beach. The opposition says the answer is more enforcement of existing laws with added police patrols of the beach so they can continue to drink. But that means pulling even more police away from San Diego neighborhoods at a time when

> # FAST FACT
>
> Since the town of Aberystwyth, in the United Kingdom, established itself as an alcohol-free zone in 2005, street poverty and vagrancy have dropped 80 percent. Alcohol-related crimes have dropped 15 percent.

the police department is already under-staffed. The reality is that it is high time San Diegans in all of our neighborhoods stopped paying the price of less law enforcement and longer response times to accommodate the unruly drunks at the beach.

EVALUATING THE AUTHOR'S ARGUMENTS:

SafeBeaches.org uses logic, reasoning, and facts to make its argument that alcohol bans benefit society. It does not, however, use any quotations to support its point. If you were to rewrite this viewpoint and insert quotations, what authorities or voices might you quote from? Where would you place these quotations to bolster the points SafeBeaches.org makes?

Alcohol Bans Hurt Society

Eric Christiansen

"[Don't make] businesses and the 99.9 percent of the populace that drank responsibly suffer the consequences of a unilateral and complete alcohol beach ban."

In the following viewpoint author Eric Christiansen argues that alcohol bans hurt small business owners and thus the entire community. He discusses the repercussions of a 2008 decision to ban alcohol on San Diego beaches. Although fewer alcohol-related incidents and arrests occurred, Christiansen says hundreds of thousands of people skipped coming to the beach entirely. This meant that bars, restaurants, surf shops, retail stores, markets, vacation rentals, and other tourism-related businesses all suffered as a result. He concludes that businesses cannot afford a total ban on alcohol, especially given the current recession.

Christiansen lives in Serra Mesa, San Diego, and co-owns a restaurant in Mission Beach.

AS YOU READ, CONSIDER THE FOLLOWING QUESTIONS:

1. How many fewer people does Christiansen say visited San Diego beaches on Memorial Day in 2008 compared to 2007?

The San Diego Union-Tribune, June 8, 2008 for "Alcohol Beach Ban Punishes Businesses," by Eric Christiansen. Reproduced by permission of the author.

2. By what percent was business down for some small-business owners in 2008, according to Christiansen?
3. List three suggestions the author makes for keeping alcohol legal on beaches but reducing the crime and rowdiness associated with it.

As a small-business owner in Mission Beach [San Diego], every year I greatly look forward to the arrival of the tourist season. Without such a yearly boost in sales, I would not be able to make a living.

Every year, more and more vacation rentals replace residents of condos, apartments and homes who in the past had lived in Mission Beach year-round. That in itself has made my restaurant business, and many others in Mission Beach, really rely on the summer months to make money, save it away and hope to make it through the much slower "off-season." Now that our economy may be in a recession, with gas prices steadily rising, causing the cost of all goods to rise, it is even harder to make any profits at all.

Compounding all of this was the decision to completely alter the beach by imposing the zero-tolerance alcohol ban on San Diego beaches.

Less Booze, Less Business

This year's [2008] spring break was virtually non-existent. I was told that letters were sent to Arizona residents as well as ads taken out in college papers there to inform them of the 180-degree change in alcohol policy. Well, they got the memo, and though many families came to Mission Beach, vacation rentals were for the first time in many years not sold out, and the swarms of students that normally come out to spend all of their money, or more likely their parents', went elsewhere.

Even more evident was the huge decrease in visitors and vacationers over the recent Memorial Day weekend. Parking lots were half full, traffic was minimal and the beaches were virtually empty in comparison with past years.

According to a statistic published in the *Union-Tribune* on May 28 [2008], 234,261 people visited San Diego County beaches over the three-day weekend compared with 630,450 visitors the prior year. That's nearly 400,000 fewer people, a 63 percent decrease. Some blamed it on "May gray" [weather] and the price of gas. While gas prices are astronomical, driving from [the surrounding suburbs of] Escondido, El Cajon, Chula Vista, etc., certainly won't break the bank. I was at the beach working the entire holiday weekend, and though that Friday and early Saturday the area suffered from poor weather; from Saturday afternoon on, the weather was great!

Fewer Tourists Hurt Businesses

Unbelievably, the San Diego media machine has barely mentioned the effect the beach-alcohol ban has had on day-trippers and tourists alike.

Restaurants, mom-and-pop markets, surf shops, retail stores, vacation rentals, etc., all depend upon the crowds that descend on San Diego's beaches every summer. Residents will tout the decrease in crime and alleviation of summer/tourist-induced traffic woes. San Diego's No. 1 industry, however, is tourism. We have fabulous weather, beautiful beaches and a city with many attractions that cater to tourism. Without that money, our city would undoubtedly fall deeper into financial trouble.

Ask yourself this: How many barbecues have you attended where there haven't been beer or wine served? Quite honestly, a barbecue isn't a barbecue without a few adult beverages consumed responsibly among friends. It is unfortunate a few bad apples caused a knee-jerk reaction that was made without any economic impact analysis.

> **FAST FACT**
>
> According to the National Highway Traffic Safety Administration, in 2007 the alcohol-impaired driving fatality rate per 100 million vehicle miles of travel decreased to 0.43—the lowest on record.

If this Memorial Day weekend was an indicator of what the rest of the summer will be like, many businesses are going to suffer, and some won't make it at all. I've spoken with several small-business owners, and some have stated that they are down 70 percent from last year.

The ban on alcohol at San Diego beaches has resulted in fewer tourists, and local businesses are suffering.

Zero-Tolerance Has Hurt the Whole City

The alcohol ban is to be re-evaluated at the end of the year. Undoubtedly, we will see fewer alcohol incidents, accidents and arrests, but equally so will be the decrease in tourism that San Diego so heavily depends upon. I recognize that the way our beaches operated prior to the ban created many alcohol-related problems and issues. A change was absolutely necessary, but a zero-tolerance stance has many repercussions other than lowering alcohol-related incidents and lessening traffic. Perhaps a compromise can be made.

The city could stringently limit the hours that alcohol can be consumed on the beaches, say 1 to 7 p.m. Create "Family Friendly Zones" where alcohol is banned, and families can safely enjoy the beach (much like the swimming/surfing zones).

Do Not Punish Everyone

Increase fines and penalties for alcohol-related incidents. Increase police presence in areas more renowned as trouble spots. Areas on the East Coast implemented a permit system so that people wishing to hold a barbecue with beer can purchase a permit for a nominal fee. That person is then responsible for his or her group.

These are just suggestions, but I state them in hopes that an educated dialogue can be had that looks at a way to make our beaches safer and more friendly to all people, without making businesses and the 99.9 percent of the populace that drank responsibly suffer the consequences of a unilateral and complete alcohol beach ban.

EVALUATING THE AUTHORS' ARGUMENTS:

Eric Christiansen disagrees with the authors of the previous viewpoint on whether alcohol should be banned in public spaces like beaches. After reading both viewpoints, with which perspective do you ultimately agree? Why? List at least three pieces of evidence that swayed you.

Viewpoint

5

Restricting Alcohol Advertising Would Benefit Society

Peter Anderson

"Young people are particularly vulnerable to alcohol and to alcohol advertising, which is commonly targeted to them."

Peter Anderson is a public health consultant who lives in Spain. In the following viewpoint he presents evidence for why some forms of alcohol advertising should be banned. Anderson explains that young people are very vulnerable to alcohol advertisings—exposure to ads on television, in magazines, and through other media encourages them to start drinking and to drink heavily. But when they do, they are more prone to drunk driving, death, injury, suicide, depression, fighting, unprotected sex, and other problems. Anderson argues that if young people could be protected from these problems, all of society would benefit. Therefore, alcohol ads targeting young people should be restricted.

Children and adolescents have greater vulnerability to the harmful effects of alcohol than adults. As well as usually being physically smaller, they lack experience of drinking and its effects. They have no context or reference point for assessing or regulating their drinking, and, furthermore, they have built up no tolerance to alcohol. From mid-adolescence to early adulthood there are major increases in the amount and frequency of alcohol consumption and alcohol-related problems. Those with heavier consumption in their mid-teens tend to be those with heavier consumption, alcohol dependence and alcohol-related harm, including poorer mental health, poorer education outcome and increased risk of crime in early adulthood.

During adolescence, alcohol can lead to structural changes in the hippocampus (a part of the brain involved in the learning process) and at high levels can permanently impair brain development. Drinking by adolescents and young adults is associated with automobile crash injury and death, suicide and depression, missed classes and decreased academic performance, loss of memory, blackouts, fighting, property damage, peer criticism and broken friendships, date rape, and unprotected sexual intercourse that places people at risk for sexually transmitted diseases, HIV infection and unplanned pregnancy.

Alcohol Ads Encourage Underage Drinking

Alcohol advertising is one of the many factors that have the potential to encourage youth drinking. For young people who have not started

Children Remember Alcohol Ads

A study by the Rand Corporation looked at the effects of alcohol advertising on children. It found that fourth and ninth graders who watched beer ads featuring animated animals and soda ads featuring young girls remembered the brand names more often than when shown age-appropriate beer commercials targeted toward adults.

Students Who Correctly Named the Brand in the Edited TV Ads

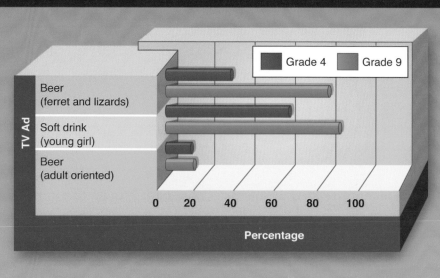

Taken from: Rand Corporation, "Forging the Link Between Alcohol Advertising and Underage Drinking," 2006. www.rand.org/pubs/research_briefs/2006/RAND_RB9073.pdf.

to drink, expectancies are influenced by normative assumptions about teenage drinking as well as through the observation of drinking by parents, peers, and models in the mass media. Research has linked exposure to portrayals of alcohol use in the mass media with the development of positive drinking expectancies by children and adolescents. Young people with more positive affective responses to alcohol advertising hold more favourable drinking expectancies, perceive greater social approval for drinking, believe drinking is more common among peers and adults, and intend to drink more as adults. All these beliefs interact to produce a greater likelihood of drinking, or of intention to drink within the near future.

Alcohol Ads Increase Youth Drinking

A recent systematic review to assess the impact of alcohol advertising and media exposure on future adolescent alcohol use identified thirteen . . . studies that followed up a total of over 38,000 young people. Twelve of the thirteen studies concluded an impact of exposure on subsequent alcohol use, including initiation of drinking and heavier drinking amongst existing drinkers. . . . The thirteenth study, which tested the impact of outdoor advertising placed near schools, failed to detect an impact on alcohol use, but found an impact on intentions to use.

For example, [researcher P.L.] Ellickson *et al.* examined the relationship between a range of advertisement exposures over the course of one year and subsequent drinking among US adolescents age 12 to 13 years followed-up for at least two years, and assessed whether exposure to a prevention programme mitigated any such relationship. Forty eight per cent of 1206 grade 7 non-drinkers consumed alcohol during the previous year at grade 9. . . . Controlling for exposure to all different types of advertising as well as the impact of the prevention programme, exposure to beer concession stands at sports or music events predicted drinking onset for non-drinkers in the previous 12 months. Seventy seven per cent of 1905 grade 7 drinkers consumed alcohol in the previous year at grade 9. Again, controlling for exposure to all different types of advertising as well as the impact of the prevention programme, exposure to beer concession stands at sports or music events predicted frequency of drinking amongst existing drinkers in the previous 12 months, as did exposure to magazines with alcohol advertisements. Similarly, [R.C.] Collins *et al.* . . . evaluated the impact of exposure of alcohol marketing on beer use amongst 1786 grade 6 students (11–12 years olds) one year later. The joint effect of exposure to advertisements . . . were significant. Twenty

> ## FAST FACT
>
> The hard liquor industry voluntarily prevented its own advertisements from being broadcast on radio (in 1936) and on television (in 1948). Beginning in the late 1990s it started to ease this ban, and more liquor ads began appearing on television.

per cent of youth in the 75th percentile of alcohol marketing exposure at grade 6 reported past year beer drinking at grade 7, compared with 13% in the 25th percentile. . . .

Ads Should Be Banned, Not Voluntarily Removed

In several European countries, there is a reliance on "self-regulation"—voluntary systems implemented by economic operators, including advertising, media and alcohol producers. However, evidence from a number of studies shows that these voluntary systems do not prevent the kind of marketing which has an impact on younger people and that self-regulation seems to work only to the extent that there is a current and credible threat of regulation by government. For example, in Australia, following a formal review in 2003, the Ministerial Council on Drug Strategy proposed a revised Alcoholic Beverages Advertising Code (ABAC), which came into operation in 2004. From May 2004 until March 2005 television and magazine advertising campaigns were monitored for alcohol products. Over this period 14 complaints against alcohol advertisements were lodged with the self-regulatory board, and the study authors recruited an independent expert panel to assess the advertisements and complaints. In eight of the 14 cases a majority of the judges perceived the advertisement to be in breach of the code, and in no cases did a majority perceive no breach. Conversely, however, none of the complaints were upheld by the Advertising Standards Board (ASB).

The Public Supports Stricter Regulations

A 2006 Eurobarometer survey found that 76% of the European Union population would approve the banning of alcohol advertising targeting young people in all Member States. Every second respondent (50%) said that they "agree totally" with this idea. A country-by-country analysis shows that in all polled countries the majority of respondents would favour such a ban, with 71% of the UK population agreeing. . . .

Using data from international time-series analyses, the World Health Organization's CHOICE project modelled the impact of an advertising ban in the European Union. The model estimated that a ban on advertising implemented throughout the Union could prevent

5% of all alcohol-related ill-health, at an overall cost of 95 million [euros] each year. With a cost effectiveness ratio of 500 [euros] per year of ill-health and premature mortality prevented in western Europe, an advertising ban would be about half as cost effective as a tax increase (241 [euros]), but nearly four times as cost effective as an early identification and brief advice programme in primary care (1959 [euros]).

We Should Protect the Vulnerable

Young people are particularly vulnerable to alcohol and to alcohol advertising, which is commonly targeted to them. Alcohol advertisements are related to young people's expectancies about alcohol and their desire to consume alcohol, and a recent systematic review has found evidence that alcohol advertisements increase the likelihood of

Studies show alcohol advertising influences young people to start drinking and, once drinking, to drink heavily.

young people starting to drink, the amount they drink, and the amount they drink on any one occasion. Experience demonstrates that it is possible to regulate commercial communications in both traditional and non-traditional media, with, for example, the European Union 2003 tobacco directive banning the advertising of tobacco products in the broadcast and print media, and relevant sport sponsorship. Thus, it is feasible to ban alcohol advertising, which, for advertising targeting young people, would be supported by three quarters of European citizens.

EVALUATING THE AUTHOR'S ARGUMENTS:

To make his argument that some forms of alcohol advertising should be banned, Anderson says that countries cannot rely on "self-regulation" to reduce the number of alcohol ads seen by children. What do you think he means by this? Explain your answer in two or three sentences.

Alcohol Advertising Should Not Be Restricted

Cameron Jones

> *"Throwing up a few signs in an already alcohol-rich environment is not going to cause any extra damage."*

In the following viewpoint student Cameron Jones argues that alcohol advertising should not be restricted, especially when it could bring much-needed money to schools and colleges. He discusses how the University of Arizona has refused to let alcohol be advertised at campus sporting events. But Jones says such advertising could bring in hundreds of thousands of dollars that would benefit the school. In Jones's opinion, banning the ads does not achieve anything—students are going to drink regardless of whether they see alcohol ads. Jones therefore concludes it is a mistake for schools to pass up alcohol advertising dollars and that such advertising does no harm.

AS YOU READ, CONSIDER THE FOLLOWING QUESTIONS:

1. According to Jones, how much does the University of Missouri receive each year from Anheuser-Busch ads?

2. How much does Jones say the University of Wisconsin receives from Anheuser-Busch and Miller to advertise on campus?
3. What compromise does Jones suggest for dealing with the issue of alcohol on campus?

The University of Arizona [UA] is eschewing hundreds of thousands of dollars in an era of unprecedented budget shortfalls and tuition hikes.

Giving Ad Dollars Away

The reason: The UA athletics department has a strict policy in place restricting the sale of alcohol at campus sporting events and does not allow alcohol companies to advertise in any of its arenas or stadiums. "Our values are such that we're not going to sell our souls for the almighty dollar," said Jim Livengood, UA athletic director.

But as the financial crisis across campus worsens, it can be questioned whether that policy needs to be re-evaluated, especially given the fact that so much money would be available should the university decide to go in that direction.

For example, Pacific 10 Conference rival USC [University of Southern California] stopped selling alcohol at football games before the 2005 season, but in 2004 the school made more than $700,000 from alcohol sales. There are 18 Division I colleges that allow the sale of alcohol on their campuses at athletic events.

Because fans are going to drink beforehand, either at home or while tailgating, not selling alcohol on campus effectively cuts the university out of a very profitable market. [UA] is essentially diverting those customers and their money to the convenience stores and supermarkets around the school.

Alcohol Ad Money Can Help Schools

The administration appears steadfast in its stance against selling alcohol at games, despite the potential profits. "I think it's so inappropriate to have a university in the business of selling alcohol that I just can't see that happening," UA President Robert Shelton said.

The school's policy prohibits the use of university funds to purchase alcoholic beverages. If the school can't buy alcohol, then it can't sell it at athletic events, so any change in mindset would first require a change in policy.

But given the university's financial woes, a model similar to that of the University of Missouri's with Anheuser-Busch or the University of Wisconsin's with both Miller and Busch could strike a reasonable balance. Missouri receives $490,000 a year from Anheuser-Busch, while Miller and Busch pay Wisconsin a combined total of $450,000 annually to advertise on its campus.

Similarly, the University of Colorado receives $392,000 a year from Coors Brewing Co. The school's 11,000-seat basketball arena also bears the Coors name, thanks to a $5 million gift from the company.

Of those schools, only Colorado allows the sale of alcohol on its campus. Missouri and Wisconsin allow alcohol companies to advertise but not distribute. Such relationships aren't unprecedented in college athletics, so why doesn't [UA] have one?

Standing in the Way of Profits

The school's policy on alcohol states that advertising and sponsorships from alcoholic beverage distributors are acceptable, but no

The University of Wisconsin makes about $450,000 per year by allowing beer companies to advertise on campus.

reference to the alcoholic product is permitted, thus eliminating any incentive for those companies to advertise, said Scott MacKenzie, the assistant athletics director for marketing and corporate sales at UA. That means Golden Eagle Distributing Corporation could advertise without making any reference to Anheuser-Busch, the company [for] which Golden Eagle distributes alcohol.

Also, the fact that the Pac-10 allows alcohol companies to advertise during radio broadcasts of UA sporting events can send a mixed message to students. Furthermore, a large percentage of fans at [UA] sporting events have no affiliation to the university. The substantial number of fans with gray hair inside McKale Center on game days indicates that the school could allow alcohol companies to advertise without being accused of targeting students.

From a financial standpoint, those restrictions seem to be the only thing in the way of very large profits for the university. "If those rules ever changed, there would certainly be several beer companies at the table," said MacKenzie.

Shelton, for his part, does not dismiss the idea of one day entering into a partnership with an alcoholic beverage company. "I would be open to a discussion," he said, "but again, policy would dictate the type of ad that you would have."

And if that policy were to change? "The key is finding the right partner and making sure that your own, our own, policies and principles aren't compromised," Shelton said. "And when alcohol is involved, you have just a few extra things to think about." But that is a gray area the university would prefer not to enter.

Shelton mentioned that although universities have been successful in changing the less-than-desirable traits of their sponsors in the past—Nike's labor practices in Asia, for example—this is a different situation. The issue with alcohol companies isn't how they make their product, he said; it is the product itself. "I would rather look other places than alcohol," Shelton said. "I'm not a puritan. I enjoy a glass of wine, but I just think that there are so many more potential sponsors that fit well with the goals of the university."

Students Are Going to Drink Regardless

If the university was completely against alcohol that would be one thing; it should not compromise its values for a few dollars.

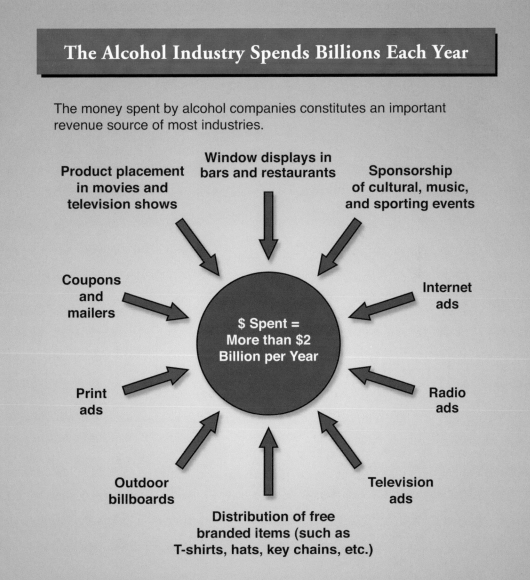

The Alcohol Industry Spends Billions Each Year

The money spent by alcohol companies constitutes an important revenue source of most industries.

Product placement in movies and television shows

Window displays in bars and restaurants

Sponsorship of cultural, music, and sporting events

Coupons and mailers

Internet ads

$ Spent = More than $2 Billion per Year

Print ads

Radio ads

Outdoor billboards

Distribution of free branded items (such as T-shirts, hats, key chains, etc.)

Television ads

But Pandora's Box is already open, as alcohol is everywhere during UA tailgating festivities. This is college, so throwing up a few signs in an already alcohol-rich environment is not going to cause any extra damage.

The school could certainly use the money, and selling just advertisements, not alcohol, is a compromise that could help meet some of the school's needs financially while still maintaining the university's image. The university should not underestimate the maturity of its students.

Taking some easy money is the route to go. Students can deal with a sign telling them something they already see everywhere else.

EVALUATING THE AUTHORS' ARGUMENTS:

Cameron Jones, the author of this viewpoint, and Peter Anderson, author of the previous viewpoint, disagree on whether alcohol advertisements are harmless. State each author's position. With which author's perspective do you agree? Explain why.

Chapter 2

Should the Drinking Age Be Lowered?

Students at the University of Kansas advocate lowering the state's drinking age to eighteen. Drinking age controversies have been around since the end of Prohibition.

Viewpoint

1

The Drinking Age Should Be Lowered to Eighteen

Pateik Dalmia

"We wouldn't give 16 year-olds a driver's license without first teaching them to drive safely. Yet this is our approach to teenage drinking."

The drinking age should be lowered to eighteen, argues Pateik Dalmia in the following viewpoint. The current drinking age has not helped the United States avoid its problems with alcohol, he notes. Americans are more dependent on alcohol and binge drink more often than people in countries with lower drinking ages, he says. This is because Americans are not taught to drink alcohol responsibly. Dalmia thinks a lowered drinking age would help young people become comfortable with moderate alcohol use, which would discourage them from becoming overly dependent on alcohol, from binge drinking in secret, and from drunk driving. Dalmia concludes that lowering the drinking age is the best way to keep young people safe.

Dalmia writes opinion articles for the *Johns Hopkins News-Letter*, from which this viewpoint was taken.

AS YOU READ, CONSIDER THE FOLLOWING QUESTIONS:
  1. According to Dalmia, what is the rate of alcohol dependence in the United States? What is it in Italy and Spain?
  2. What does Dwight Heath of Brown University say about kids who drink alcohol with their parents?
  3. How does Dalmia say European countries handle the problem of drunk driving among young people?

C an you think of a country in which 80 percent of its citizens have committed a misdemeanor by the time they are in the 12th grade? If you thought of the United States, you are right! Before graduating from high school, 80 percent of Americans have drunk alcohol and 62.3 percent have been inebriated according to teenhelp.com.

Setting the legal drinking age at 21, the highest in the world, has made criminals out of an overwhelming majority. So what's the solution? Stricter enforcement of the law until people finally give in? This is the failing method the government has resorted to for the past two decades, and it is time for a new approach. It is time we caught up with the rest of the world and revised our failing alcohol policies.

Despite High Drinking Age, Alcohol Is a Problem

So why is the U.S. unique in its unusually high drinking age? Advocates of the current drinking age often argue that starting at a younger age makes one more likely to become an alcoholic later in life. There might be some scientific truth to this. However, alcoholism is a far greater problem in the U.S. than in other countries with more lenient alcohol policies.

As anthropologist Dwight Heath has pointed out, Italy and Spain report very low rates of alcohol dependence: less than 1 percent in Italy and 2.8 percent in Spain. In the U.S. the rate is 7.8 percent. What explains this alarmingly higher rate of alcohol dependence in the U.S.?

Teach Responsibility, Not Prohibition

One answer is that because American teenagers are not allowed to legally drink, they are forced to do it in secret. Without adult

International Drinking Ages

The United States has one of the highest drinking ages in the whole world.

No Official Drinking Age

Albania	Equatorial Guinea	Guinea-Bissau	Kyrgyzstan
Cambodia	Gabon	Jamaica	Morocco
Comoros	Ghana	Kazakhstan	Togo

16–18

Algeria	Czech Republic	Lesotho	Seychelles
Argentina	Denmark	Lithuania	Singapore
Australia	Dominican	Luxembourg	Slovenia
Austria	Republic	Malawi	South Africa
Azerbaijan	Ecuador	Malta	Spain
Bahamas	El Salvador	Mauritius	Sri Lanka
Belarus	Eritrea	Mexico	Swaziland
Belgium	Estonia	Mongolia	Sweden
Belize	Ethiopia	Mozambique	Switzerland
Bolivia	Finland	Namibia	Tajikistan
Botswana	France	Netherlands	Thailand
Brazil	Georgia	New Zealand	Tonga
Bulgaria	Germany	Niger	Trinidad and
Burundi	Greece	Nigeria	Tobago
Canada	Guatemala	North Korea	Turkey
Cape Verde	Guyana	Norway	Turkmenistan
Central African	Hungary	Panama	Uganda
Republic	Iraq	Papua New	Ukraine
Chile	Ireland	Guinea	United Kingdom
China	Israel	Peru	Uruguay
Colombia	Italy	Philippines	Vanuatu
Congo	Jordan	Portugal	Venezuela
Costa Rica	Kenya	Russia	Zambia
Croatia	Latvia	Rwanda	Zimbabwe
Cyprus	Lebanon	Samoa	

19–20

Iceland	South Korea	Paraguay	
Japan	Nicaragua		

21 or Older

Egypt	Indonesia	Palau	United Arab
Fiji	Micronesia	Solomon Islands	Emirates
India	N. Mariana Islands	United States	

Alcohol Is Illegal

Afghanistan	Gambia	Libya	Saudi Arabia
Bangladesh	Iran	Pakistan	Yemen
Brunei	Kuwait	Sudan	

Taken from: International Center for Alcohol Policies (ICAP), www.icap.org.

supervision, it is obvious that a teenager will drink in excess. We wouldn't give 16 year-olds a driver's license without first teaching them to drive safely. Yet this is our approach to teenage drinking.

In France, teenagers often enjoy a glass of wine at the dinner table. Their first meeting with alcohol isn't at a binge-promoting frat party but rather under the watchful guidance of their parents.

"Kids who drank with their parents were about half as likely to say they had drunk alcohol in the past month and one-third as likely to say they had had five or more consecutive drinks in the previous two weeks," said Dwight Heath, a professor of Anthropology at Brown University, in an interview.

In the U.S. a parent can be imprisoned for allowing his teenager to drink at a party—a party that the teenager will be going to anyway.

Because American teenagers typically first encounter alcohol without adult supervision, the frequency of teenage alcohol abuse is staggering. The Center on Alcohol Marketing and Youth reports that 96 percent of the alcohol drunk by 15 to 20 year-olds is consumed when the drinker is having five or more drinks at a time.

> ## FAST FACT
>
> The United States is one of four countries with a minimum legal drinking age of twenty-one. The only countries with stricter laws are Islamic ones in which alcohol is completely illegal.

According to the Century Council, an organization aimed at fighting underage drinking, in 2006 40 percent of college students reported "binge-drinking" within two weeks of taking the survey. If we do not lower the drinking age altogether, we should, at a minimum, make it legal for parents to casually introduce their teenagers to alcohol.

Let Teens Learn to Drink First

The other argument that defenders of the current drinking age make is that teenagers should not be allowed to begin drinking at the same time they obtain their driver's license. They fear that teenagers will take advantage of the new freedoms at the same time. Although not limited to teenagers, in 2007 31.7 percent of traffic fatalities

Teenagers in France can drink beer at the age of sixteen. Some argue this helps them develop a responsible relationship with alcohol.

involved alcohol, according to the National Highway Traffic Safety Administration.

Several European countries have solved this problem by having a lower drinking age than driving age (the usual drinking age is 16 and the usual driving age is 18). By the time European teenagers can drive they are habituated and responsible.

As a result, the auto-fatality rate per capita in England is half that of the United States, according to Professor M.R. Franks of Southern University. The other thing that makes safe drinking possible in Europe is better public transportation. Perhaps, instead of fighting inevitable underage drinking, we should make it easier for citizens to avoid driving altogether by providing other means of transportation.

Prohibition Never Works

The lesson to be learned is the same lesson that we learned during Prohibition, when a Constitutional Amendment outlawing the sale and transportation of alcohol was enacted. Prohibition did not achieve its goal of deterring alcohol consumption, and instead a black market for alcohol thrived. Prohibition soon became the only Constitutional Amendment to ever be repealed.

The lesson, as *Reason* Magazine's writer Radley Balko points out, is: "State and local governments are far better at passing laws that reflect the values, morals and habits of their communities."

EVALUATING THE AUTHOR'S ARGUMENTS:

Dalmia claims that a surefire way to encourage a dangerous behavior is to outlaw it. What does he mean by this? With what historical evidence does he support his claim? After answering these questions, state whether you agree with him on this point.

The Drinking Age Should Not Be Lowered to Eighteen

"The decrease in the drinking age brought about an increase in alcohol traffic fatalities and injuries."

Mothers Against Drunk Driving

In the following viewpoint Mothers Against Drunk Driving argues against lowering the drinking age to 18. The authors say that a lowered drinking age results in more youth drinking, which in turn results in more drunk driving fatalities and injuries. They discuss the 1970s and early 1980s, when the drinking age was lowered to 18, 19, or 20 in twenty-nine states. But problems with youth drinking became so bad that sixteen states voluntarily raised their drinking age after just a few years. Since the minimum legal drinking age has been set at 21, the authors claim more than twenty-five thousand lives have been saved. For these reasons, they oppose lowering the drinking age and suggest alternative ways to reduce binge and youth drinking.

Mothers Against Drunk Driving was founded by Candy Lightner in 1980 after her daughter, Cari, was killed by a drunk driver. The organization's goal is to reduce drunk driving, prevent underage drinking, and support drunk driving victims.

AS YOU READ, CONSIDER THE FOLLOWING QUESTIONS:
1. What are "blood borders," as described by the authors?
2. How many lives per year do the authors say are saved by having a drinking age of 21?
3. By what percent does a minimum legal drinking age of 21 reduce traffic fatalities, according to the Centers for Disease Control?

History speaks for itself and the history of the 21 minimum drinking age law is no exception. As one of the nation's most scrutinized laws, there is a wealth of data on the law's effectiveness and why it works. And it is the history of that law that best illustrates that fact.

A Lower Drinking Age Brought Death and Injury

For almost 40 years, most states voluntarily set their minimum drinking age law at 21. But at the height of the Vietnam War in the early 1970s, 29 states began lowering their drinking age to more closely align with the newly reduced military enlistment and voting age. And of those 29 states, no uniformity in age limits— drinking ages varied from 18 to 20 and sometimes even varied based on the type of alcohol being consumed (e.g. 18 for beer, 20 for liquor).

The results of this "natural experiment" were fairly immediate and hard to miss: The decrease in the drinking age brought about an increase in alcohol traffic fatalities and injuries. So much so that, by 1983, 16 states voluntarily raised their drinking age back to 21—a move that brought about an immediate decrease in drinking and driving traffic fatalities incidents.

Some states, however, kept a lower drinking age. This created a patchwork of states with varied drinking ages that led to what was known as "blood borders." They were called blood borders because teens would drive across state lines, drink and then drive back home across state lines killing and injuring themselves and others.

Around this time, the nation began taking a firm stance on the issue of drunk driving. And because it was apparent that a 21 drinking age law reduced alcohol-related fatalities and injuries, there was a groundswell to help decrease drunk driving deaths and injuries by raising the minimum drinking age to 21. President Ronald Reagan responded to growing evidence that a 21 drinking age law would save lives.

On July 17, 1984, President Reagan signed into law the Uniform Drinking Age Act mandating all states to adopt 21 as the legal drinking age within five years. By 1988, all states had set 21 as the minimum drinking age, which is where it should remain.

The 21 Age Law Saves Lives and Reduces Youth Drinking

Since that time, the 21 minimum drinking age law has saved about 900 lives per year as estimated by the National Traffic Highway Administration (NHTSA). In short, there are more than 25,000 people alive today since all states adopted the law in 1988. That's about as many people in a sold-out crowd at a professional basketball game or a medium-sized U.S. college.

FAST FACT

According to Mothers Against Drunk Driving, the minimum legal drinking age of twenty-one saves approximately nine hundred lives a year.

In fact, the 21 minimum drinking age law has been heralded as one of the most effective public safety laws ever passed. It is also one of the nation's most examined laws with countless studies that have been conducted to measure the law's effectiveness—all of which have come to the same conclusion: the law saves lives.

Youth drinking rates have also declined since the 21 age law went into effect. The 2006 *Monitoring the Future* study shows declining alcohol consumption among American youth, although alcohol use continues to be widespread among today's youth. A look at all of the

Mothers Against Drunk Drivers (MADD) founder Candy Lightner, second from left, watches President Ronald Reagan sign the Uniform Drinking Age Act on July 17, 1984. MADD has fought against lowering the drinking age since 1980.

research on the minimum drinking age from 1960 to 2000 found that the bulk of the evidence shows that 21 minimum drinking age laws decrease underage consumption of alcohol. Even over the last 15 years, after the passage of the 21 minimum drinking age laws, the percentage of 8th, 10th, and 12th graders who drank alcohol in the past year decreased 38 percent, 23 percent and 14 percent respectively.

Studies Show the 21 Minimum Drinking Age Is Better, Safer

In 2003, the Centers for Disease Control (CDC) looked at 49 high-quality, peer-reviewed studies on the effects of changing the minimum drinking age law. Almost every study found that increasing the minimum drinking age to 21 saved lives with an average decrease in traffic fatalities of 16 percent. The studies also showed that lowering the minimum drinking age to 18 or 19 caused an average increase in crashes by 8 to 10 percent.

NHTSA's study, "Determine Why There Are Fewer Young Alcohol-Impaired Drivers" found that between 1982 and 1998, there were 61 percent fewer drinking drivers involved in fatal crashes under age 21 and a 56 percent decrease among 21–24 year olds. This is against a backdrop of a decrease of only 24 percent among 25–55 year olds. There were a number of safety improvements during this time including better roads and laws, and safer cars. But because the people most directly affected by the law had the greatest decreases, NHTSA concluded "unequivocally that MLDA [minimum legal drinking age] 21 laws reduce youth drinking and driving, as measured by traffic crash involvements."

The 2006 *Monitoring the Future* study shows a decline in alcohol consumption among American youth, though alcohol remains the nation's No. 1 youth drug problem. After the passage of the 21 minimum drinking age law, the percentage of 8th, 10th, and 12th graders who drank alcohol in the past year decreased 38 percent, 23 percent, and 14 percent respectively.

Better Ways to Reduce Underage Drinking

In March 2007, the acting U.S. Surgeon General released his *Call to Action to Prevent and Reduce Underage Drinking*, which properly and methodically outlines the serious nature of underage drinking. He also provides a roadmap for communities and states to follow in order to greatly reduce the problems with underage drinking.

His recommendations include:

1. Increase enforcement of underage drinking laws
2. Properly educate parents to provide them with factual information about the dangers of adolescent alcohol use
3. Community members collaborate on partnerships and coalitions to implement effective prevention strategies

4. Having universities examine their policies and practices to ensure they are sending a strong message that underage alcohol use is illegal
5. Decrease accessibility of alcohol to those under 21
6. Ensure the judicial system is properly enforcing laws
7. Decrease the amount of alcohol advertisement reaching a youth audience

EVALUATING THE AUTHORS' ARGUMENTS:

Mothers Against Drunk Driving claims that keeping the drinking age at 21 saves lives. But the previous author, Pateik Dalmia, claims lowering the age to 18 will save lives. After reading both viewpoints, whom do you think is right? Why? List at least three pieces of evidence that helped you make up your mind.

Lowering the Drinking Age Will Reduce Binge Drinking in College

The Las Vegas Sequitur

"[Kids] could learn moderation from their parents rather than trying to glean it from the encouraging paddle of a fraternity pledge master."

The following viewpoint was written by editors at the *Sequitur*, a newspaper in Las Vegas. They argue that lowering the drinking age to seventeen will reduce binge drinking, which is a huge problem on college campuses. Because teenagers have no experience with alcohol, they tend to overindulge once they get to college. But binge drinking is dangerous and results in violence, sexual assault, injury, and even death. Lowering the drinking age would help young people get comfortable with alcohol before they go to college, claim the authors, and many college presidents agree with them. The authors conclude that the high-pressure college environment is not a good place for young people to first learn about alcohol, and so the drinking age should be lowered to promote responsible drinking early on.

AS YOU READ, CONSIDER THE FOLLOWING QUESTIONS:
1. What is the Amethyst Initiative, and how does it factor into the authors' argument?
2. What is the "forbidden fruit phenomenon," according to the authors?
3. What punishment do the authors suggest for those caught violating a lowered drinking age?

Once beyond the auspices of home, 18 year olds rush to alcohol like beer leaving a funnel: quickly and messily. Underage drinking has become such a problem that many want to reconsider the legal drinking age. They want it lowered, and we agree.

A powerful movement known as the Amethyst Initiative, which advocates a lower drinking age to curb the "culture of dangerous binge drinking," has been signed by 129 university officials. Schools like Duke, Dartmouth, Tufts, Johns Hopkins and Amherst have witnessed firsthand that there is a definite problem in their midst—they are not responding to nothing. The best evidence agrees: binge drinking is a problem, and it is getting worse.

Treat Young People as Adults

Who is surprised? Many pundits have identified the forbidden fruit phenomenon, where the illicit quality of a controlled substance makes it all the more appealing to our human nature. We would also like to point out the buy-a-lot, drink-a-lot phenomenon, where underage Adams and Eves buy in bulk when they find the rare chance and then consume in bulk during that rare chance.

There is also the issue of trust. People act like you treat them, and treating below-21s like they cannot handle alcohol responsibly makes them think they do not have to handle it responsibly. What is a youth supposed to do with the mixed message that they can take enough responsibility for their actions to join the military, vote or be executed for murder but not drink a single beer?

Lowering the drinking age would eliminate the forbidden fruit phenomenon, the buy-a-lot, drink-a-lot phenomenon and the perception of mistrust—at least for the age groups who would then be allowed to purchase alcohol.

Kids Should Learn About Alcohol at Home, Not at College

We suggest a drinking age of 17, giving the oldest of youths the opportunity to encounter legal alcohol within the relative safety of their own home. They could learn moderation from their parents rather than trying to glean it from the encouraging paddle of a fraternity pledge master. If they overindulge, let the first toilet they spend all night worshiping be feet away from where their parents sleep.

There is vast opposition to this kind of policy change. *The Los Angeles Times* calls it "misguided"; *The Boston Herald* suggests that the academics supporting this measure are playing "pretend" if they think it will do any good. *Slate* offers compelling evidence that the dangers of alcohol consumption were diminished when the age limit was first raised to 21.

Proponents of lowering the drinking age say it will substantially reduce college binge drinking.

But it is too simplistic a view of the evidence to conclude that a higher drinking age is a better law. Even Prohibition began by successfully diminishing alcohol consumption and alcohol-related deaths—and we all know how that eventually turned out.

The Problem Is Not Drinking, but Drinking Irresponsibly

Indeed the current prohibition has been an impressive failure, especially on college campuses. (Trust us.)

Our current policy is too general. It targets and punishes the act of drinking itself, which is not itself a problem. The problem is when drinking is unmoderated or combined with various dangerous activities, such as driving. So we additionally propose coupling a lowered drinking age with strengthened penalties for those who violate the new law and especially for those who do so while doing something stupid.

For instance, those caught drinking under the lowered age, whatever it is, should lose something both valuable and appropriate to the offense, like six to 12 months added to the age at which they are entitled to a driver's license. Offenders who already have a license could simply lose it.

Finally, those who sell alcohol to kids under the proposed legal age could be punished similarly to the way they are today; fines, closures, loss of licenses, jail time, etc.

> **FAST FACT**
>
> As of 2009, representatives from 135 colleges and universities had signed the Amethyst Initiative, a movement of college and university chancellors and presidents who think lowering the legal drinking age to eighteen will reduce binge drinking on campus.

The idea is for these laws to unambiguously associate drinking with not driving and otherwise be specifically tailored to what we should be worried about—inappropriate, immoderate alcohol use. In order to prevent specific problems, it is no longer enough simply to say that drinking itself is the problem.

College Presidents Support a Lower Drinking Age

States all have the freedom to implement such a change today—but they risk federal punishment in the form of a 10 percent deduction

Consequences of Binge Drinking

Binge drinking is a growing problem on college campuses, one that has many consequences for students.

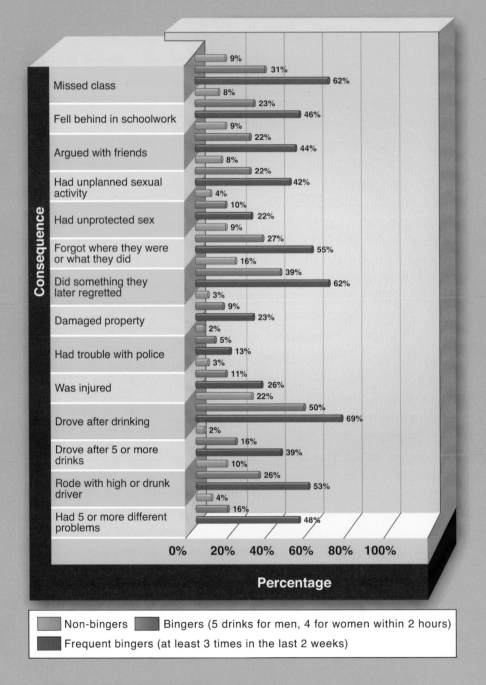

Taken from: Harvard School of Public Health, 2009.

in transportation funds. To compensate, fines can be added to the punishments for illegal drinking. Or, the federal law which perpetuates the current mini-Prohibition can be repealed or changed. Either way, positive change should not be hamstrung by cash incentives.

The Amethyst Initiative is on to something. Though two college presidents have removed their signatures since this initiative made national news, 15 more presidents have added theirs. We propose that they step even further. If 17 year olds could learn to drink in their own homes—the same way they learned to drive—instead of in the pressure of a college environment, and stricter measures are taken to punish the deadly combination of alcohol and machines, we are confident that accidents and deaths caused by binge drinking would begin to decline.

After all, good governance isn't so different than alcohol consumption, moderation is the key.

> ## EVALUATING THE AUTHORS' ARGUMENTS:
>
> The authors use the fact that some college presidents agree with the idea to lower the drinking age as proof that it can help reduce binge drinking. What do you think? Is this a good piece of evidence to use to support their argument? Why or why not? Explain your reasoning.

Viewpoint

4

Lowering the Drinking Age Will Encourage Binge Drinking in College

Darshak Sanghavi

"The current drinking age undeniably reduces teen binge-drinking and death."

In the following viewpoint Darshak Sanghavi argues that lowering the drinking age will not reduce binge drinking—in fact, he thinks it will encourage it. Sanghavi says that binge drinking does not actually have much to do with the drinking age. Therefore, lowering the age will not have a reductive effect. In his opinion, more effective measures to combat binge drinking include restricting the purchase of large quantities of alcohol (like kegs), restricting happy hours, tightening alcohol advertising, and imposing higher taxes on alcohol. Sanghavi contends that states that employ these measures have lower rates of binge drinking. He concludes that lowering the drinking age is a well-intentioned but misguided response to the problem of binge drinking in college.

Sanghavi is a health care columnist for Slate.com, from which this viewpoint was taken. He is also chief of pediatric cardiology and assistant professor of pediatrics at the University of Massachusetts Medical School.

AS YOU READ, CONSIDER THE FOLLOWING QUESTIONS:
1. How much did underage drinking drop between 1977 and 2007?
2. What measures does Sanghavi say have helped some states achieve college bingeing rates that are half of other states?
3. How does the author refute the argument that "kids will binge drink anyway"?

Last week [in August 2008], a coalition of presidents from more than 100 colleges and universities called on authorities to consider lowering the legal drinking age. The so-called Amethyst Initiative, founded by a fed-up former president of Middlebury College, asserts that "twenty-one is not working" because the current drinking age has led to a "culture of dangerous, clandestine binge-drinking" on college campuses. "How many times," they rhetorically ask, "must we relearn the lessons of prohibition?"

These academic heavyweights—who include the presidents of institutions like Duke, Spelman, Tufts, and Johns Hopkins—believe that lowering the legal drinking age can promote more responsible alcohol use. The familiar argument is that singling out alcohol to make it off-limits is odd, since 18-year-olds may legally join the military, vote, buy cigarettes, and watch porn. Meanwhile over the past decades, binge-drinking has soared among young people. The 1984 federal law that helps determine the legal drinking age is up for renewal next year, and the college presidents believe this law "stifles meaningful debate" and discourages "new ideas" to stop binge-drinking, like allowing kids over 18 to buy alcohol after a course on its "history, culture, law, chemistry, biology, neuroscience as well as exposure to accident victims and individuals in recovery."

The Drinking Age Is Not Related to Binge Drinking

It's nice to think that simply lowering the drinking age would make college students behave better (as well as cheer loudly). But the

Amethyst Initiative—named for the gemstone believed by ancient Greeks to stave off drunkenness—has naively exaggerated the benefits of a lower legal drinking age. They ignore some of the implications of their recommendations, fail to acknowledge their own complicity in the campus drinking problem, and ultimately gloss over better solutions to bingeing. Kind of like addicts might.

In truth, the higher drinking age saves lives and has little relation to college bingeing. Some history: After her daughter was killed by an intoxicated driver, Candy Lightner founded Mothers Against Drunk Driving and successfully lobbied for the 1984 National Minimum Drinking Age Act (the law that's up for reauthorization in 2009), which gave full federal highway funds only to states that set the minimum age to purchase or consume alcohol at 21 years. Most states immediately complied, setting the stage for a national experiment.

According to the federal study *Monitoring the Future*, underage drinking dropped instantly. From 1977 to 2007, the percentage of 12th graders drinking at least monthly fell from 70 percent to 45 percent—almost immediately after the law was enacted, and lastingly. Fatal car crashes involving drunk young adults dipped 32 percent, resulting in 1,000 fewer lives lost per year. Impressively, this decrease occurred despite minimal efforts at enforcement; the mere presence of the law was protective. The relationship is likely causal. In 1999, by comparison, New Zealand lowered the drinking age from 20 to 18, and while alcohol-related crashes involving 15- to 19-year-olds subsequently fell, they declined far less than in the overall population. Today, all major public health authorities, including the American Medical Association, Centers for Disease Control, National Highway Traffic Safety Board, and surgeon general, support the higher drinking age.

We also know that kids in more permissive parts of the world don't drink more responsibly. A magisterial 760-page review from the Institute of Medicine in 2004 noted dryly, "As the committee demonstrates in this report, countries with lower drinking ages are not better off than the United States in terms of the harmful consequences of youths' drinking." Those romantic visions of Irish lasses demurely drinking a glass of ale or sophisticated French teens sipping wine just don't reflect reality.

Still, the college presidents signing the Amethyst statement aren't hallucinating about the American version of the problem: There *are* more binge drinkers on campuses today. Among college students, the percentage of "frequent-heavy" drinkers remained stable from 1977–89, at about 30 percent. However, bingeing began increasing steadily throughout the late 1990s, long after the legal age was increased.

Binge Drinking Reflects State Attitudes About Alcohol

So if we can't blame the drinking age, what's going on? It's key to understand that there are huge disparities in bingeing, depending on

"College presidents favor lower drinking age . . . ," cartoon by Dave Granlund, August 20, 2008. Copyright © Dave Granlund, www.davegranlund.com.

where you live and go to school. State bingeing rates vary three- to four-fold, with middle-American states like Michigan, Illinois, and Minnesota far outpacing coastal areas like Washington state, North Carolina, New York, and New Jersey. David Rosenbloom, a professor of public health at Boston University who studies alcohol use, told me bingeing rates at colleges even in the same city can differ dramatically.

The reasons aren't very complicated: The strongest determinants of college bingeing are weak state and campus alcohol control policies (the regulatory environment) and the presence of lots of bingeing older adults (a locale's overall drinking culture). Impressively, states that severely restrict the promotion of alcohol and its purchase in large quantities—for example, by requiring registration of keg sales, restricting happy hours and beer-pitcher sales, and regulating advertising like billboards—have half the college bingeing rate of states that don't.

Alcohol Should Be Taxed

In addition to lobbying for these kinds of local laws, college presidents could also promote alcohol education (obviously) and racial

In an effort to reduce underage drinking, many states require registration of beer keg sales.

and ethnic on-campus diversity (less obviously). As one might expect, alcohol education does help; for example, a brief educational program at the University of Washington reduced long-term binge-drinking in high-risk students. Additionally, young whites drink far more than young African-Americans and Latinos, men drink more than women, and younger students drink more than older students. When mixed, all the groups moderate their alcohol consumption; thus, colleges with greater student diversity have less bingeing across the board.

There's a faster and more effective way to reduce underage drinking—and bingeing—as well: Forget the drinking age debate and sharply increase excise taxes on beer, the preferred choice of underage drinkers. (In real dollars, taxes on liquor, and especially beer, have dropped substantially over the past 30 years.) Just as higher cigarette taxes trump all other methods of curbing smoking among young people, higher alcohol taxes stop kids from drinking too much. . . . Alcohol consumption mirrors its price.

David Rosenbloom notes that the five states with the highest beer taxes have half the binge drinking of other states. In 2004, the Institute of Medicine concluded, with characteristic understatement, that the "overall weight of the evidence" that higher taxes reduce alcohol abuse and related harm to young adults is "substantial." Just as gasoline taxes today don't fully reflect the societal costs of carbon emissions, alcohol taxes are too low, argue economists P.J. Cook and M.J. Moore, since they cover less than half of alcohol's external costs, including damage done by drunk young drivers.

Do Not Give In to Underage Drinking

Of course, in the end a lot of teens will binge-drink, no matter what the law says. But that's not an argument against making the legal age 21 years old to buy and consume it. (After all, a third of high-schoolers have smoked marijuana, and few people want to legalize it for them.) Rather, the current law is best viewed as a palliative medical treatment for an incurable condition. Chemotherapy can't cure terminal cancer, but it can make patients hurt a little less and perhaps survive a little longer. Similarly, the current drinking age undeniably reduces teen binge-drinking and death a little bit, without any bad side-effects. When there's no complete cure, though, desperate people are vulnerable to the dubious marketing hype of snake-oil peddlers—which is all the Amethyst Initiative is offering up now.

> **EVALUATING THE AUTHORS' ARGUMENTS:**
>
> The authors of this viewpoint and the previous viewpoint both agree that binge drinking among college students is a crisis. Yet they support very different solutions to the problem. Given what you know on the topic, what do you think is the best way to reduce binge drinking in college? Why?

Chapter 3

How Can Drunk Driving Be Prevented?

Everyone wants to reduce drunk driving, but there is wide divergence on whether stricter drunk driving laws are the most effective way to accomplish this.

Stricter Laws Can Reduce Drunk Driving

Center for Problem-Oriented Policing

"There is a broad range of social policy changes that can significantly reduce drunk driving."

The Center for Problem-Oriented Policing is composed of police practitioners, researchers, and universities who are dedicated to helping police more effectively address specific crime and disorder problems. In the following viewpoint the Center argues that tighter laws can help reduce drunk driving. It makes several suggestions, including raising the drinking age, conducting sobriety checkpoints, imposing stricter punishments for repeat offenders, suspending or revoking licenses, and other steps. The Center concludes that a variety of legal, social, police, and political enforcements are needed to reduce drunk driving.

AS YOU READ, CONSIDER THE FOLLOWING QUESTIONS:
1. What does the author say is the legal limit of intoxication for adult drivers in the United States?
2. How can prohibiting open alcohol containers in moving vehicles help reduce drunk driving accidents, according to the author?
3. What effect can sobriety checkpoints have on drunk driving, as reported by the author?

D rinking and driving is greatly influenced by contemporary social attitudes towards the practice. And although laws and law enforcement can help change social attitudes, the reverse is much more likely: that is, that changes in social attitudes will lead to stricter laws and law enforcement. The general trend in social attitudes—at least in the United States, Canada, Europe, Scandinavia, Australia, New Zealand, and Japan—has been toward a lessened tolerance for drinking and driving.

There is a broad range of social policy changes that can significantly reduce drunk driving—tax policy, urban planning, roadway design, vehicle safety, alcohol advertising, and emergency medical care, among others. . . .

Reducing the legal limit of per se violations. Most jurisdictions have enacted laws specifying that certain measurable levels of alcohol are per se violations of the law, irrespective of proof that the alcohol actually impaired the ability of the driver to operate the motor vehicle.

Reducing the legal limit of per se intoxication for adult drivers. Most countries and U.S. states set the level of per se intoxication at .08. The legal limits are often even lower for drivers of commercial vehicles. Reducing the legal limit of intoxication and vigorous enforcement of drunk driving laws have been shown to reduce the number of alcohol-related traffic fatalities, especially when combined with administrative license suspensions.

Reducing the legal limit of per se intoxication for repeat offenders. Some jurisdictions set lower per se intoxication levels for persons who have previously been convicted of drunk driving. There is some evidence that this is effective.

Reducing the legal limit of per se violations for underage drivers. Many countries and U.S. states have enacted laws that prohibit underage drivers from having any measurable level of alcohol in their systems (so-called zero tolerance laws). Although zero tolerance laws are usually not strictly enforced, they do appear to have some deterrent effect on young drivers. . . .

Raising the minimum legal drinking age. The legal drinking age in all U.S. states is now 21 years of age and there is evidence that these laws have helped reduce the number of underage drivers who

The Progressive Effects of Alcohol

When blood alcohol concentration reaches 0.08, a drinker is legally impaired and can be arrested for drunk driving. But even before that level is reached, a drinker experiences significant mental and physical impairments. This is why some advocate lowering the legal limit for blood alcohol concentration.

Blood Alcohol Concentration	Changes in Feelings and Personality	Physical and Mental Impairments
0.01 – 0.06	Relaxation Sense of well-being Loss of inhibition Lowered alertness Joyous	Thought Judgment Coordination Concentration
0.06 – 0.10	Blunted feelings Disinhibition Extroversion Impaired sexual pleasure	Reflexes impaired Reasoning Depth perception Distance acuity Peripheral vision Glare recovery
0.11 – 0.20	Over-expression Emotional swings Angry or sad Boisterous	Reaction time Gross motor control Staggering Slurred speech
0.21 – 0.29	Stupor Lose understanding Impaired sensations	Severe motor impairment Loss of consciousness Memory blackout
0.30 – 0.39	Severe depression Unconsciousness Death possible	Bladder function Breathing Heart rate
=> 0.40	Unconsciousness Death	Breathing Heart rate

Taken from: Virginia Tech, Campus Alcohol Abuse Prevention Center, 2009. www.alcohol.vt.edu.

are involved in alcohol-related crashes. It is likely that standardizing the minimum legal drinking age has also helped reduce the number of alcohol-related crashes that occur near the borders of states that formerly had different minimum drinking ages.

Prohibiting open alcohol containers in moving vehicles. Drinking while driving is especially risky because freshly imbibed alcohol is likely to cause maximum impairment to the driver. Prohibiting open containers in moving vehicles serves to restrict the availability of alcohol to drivers. There is some evidence that prohibiting open containers of alcohol in vehicles helps reduce the number of alcohol-related crashes. . . .

Increasing the number of police stops of suspected drunk drivers during high-risk periods. Because convincing drivers that they will get caught is perhaps the most important factor in deterring drunk driving, police should significantly increase the number of stops of suspected drunk drivers, particularly during times when the risk of drunk driving crashes is at its highest. This can be done by increasing the patrol time of officers looking for drunk drivers, streamlining the arrest process, encouraging citizens to report drunk drivers, and increasing the emphasis that is placed on drunk driving interdiction and enforcement. . . .

Conducting sobriety checkpoints. Sobriety checkpoints have been shown to reduce the incidence of drunk driving and alcohol-related crashes anywhere from 15 to 25 percent. Their use is generally supported by the public. Sobriety checkpoints can be either selective or random: that is, all drivers on a particular roadway can be checked for sobriety or only those

FAST FACT

According to the California Highway Patrol, one American life is lost every twenty-two minutes in an alcohol-related traffic collision.

who meet certain criteria. Some jurisdictions conduct them regularly; others only during special enforcement periods. To be most effective, checkpoints should be highly visible, so that drivers perceive that their risk of being stopped and arrested has increased. Police should consult with counsel to determine the legality of and conditions under which sobriety checkpoints may be conducted. . . .

Suspending or revoking driver licenses administratively. Suspending or revoking the licenses of those convicted of drunk driving is one of the most effective methods for reducing alcohol-related crashes, but its effectiveness is limited by the capacity of police and others

Sobriety checkpoints have been shown to be effective in reducing the number of alcohol-related crashes by 15 to 25 percent.

to enforce the conditions of suspension and revocation; moreover, this method is only effective, if at all, during the period of suspension or revocation. Administrative license suspensions—suspensions imposed by a licensing agency rather than by the courts—have proven more effective than judicial sanctions in some U.S. states, but not others.

Imposing graduated licensing systems for young drivers. Several U.S. states have enacted so-called graduated licensing for young drivers. Typically, these systems grant young drivers limited privileges in their early driving years, such as restricting the number of passengers, the hours of operation, the use of cell phones while driving, or the types of vehicles that may be driven. These systems have been shown to have a positive effect on young drivers' attitudes about drinking and driving, on their willingness to either drink and drive themselves or ride in vehicles with drinking drivers, and on reducing their involvement in fatal and injury crashes. . . .

Confiscating license plates from convicted drunk drivers. Confiscating the license plates of convicted drunk drivers is an effective way to discourage them from further drunk driving because it raises the probability that they will be stopped by police. Confiscation is a judicial sanction in some U.S. states and an administrative one in others. There is some evidence that confiscation of license plates would be more effective if it were more widely used and more widely publicized. Alternatively, some jurisdictions require convicted drunk drivers to display specially-marked license plates on their vehicles. . . .

Requiring convicted drunk drivers to complete alcohol assessment, counseling, or treatment programs. There is some evidence that successful completion of mandatory alcohol assessment and treatment programs can reduce the likelihood that those with clinically diagnosed alcohol problems will be rearrested for drunk driving. Depending on the quality of the program, the incidence of repeat drunk driving and alcohol-related crashes can be reduced by as much as 5 to 10 percent. There is some hope that new pharmaceutical treatments for alcoholism may also help reduce drunk driving by hard-core drunk drivers; as of yet, however, such treatments have not been widely tested. . . .

Reducing the consumption of alcohol. Reducing the total volume of alcohol consumed in a community can have a number of positive effects on public safety, including a reduction in drunk driving. This is especially true when young drivers are denied alcohol. Alcohol consumption can be reduced in a variety of ways, including:

- increasing the price of alcohol by raising taxes or prohibiting discount sales;
- restricting the number of bars and liquor stores;
- strict enforcement of the drinking age;
- regulating drink specials; and
- raising public awareness through educational campaigns.

Enforcing laws prohibiting serving minors and intoxicated persons. Enforcement of laws that are designed to prohibit serving minors and intoxicated persons in licensed establishments can help control a range of alcohol-related problems, including drunk driving. Enforcement efforts should be targeted at establishments where a high proportion of drunk drivers were last drinking. Unfortunately, such enforcement is rare in most jurisdictions, especially as it relates to serving intoxicated persons. This may be because police and other enforcement agents feel that they lack the resources to devote to this activity, perceive that provable cases are difficult to make, or are reluctant to face resistance from the restaurant and tavern industry. . . .

Providing alternative transportation options to drinking drivers. Alternative transportation options include designated drivers and free taxi or limousine rides. There is evidence that drinking drivers, even heavy drinkers, will use alternative transportation if it is made readily available. There is also evidence that alternative transportation programs can significantly reduce the incidence of drunk driving and alcohol-related traffic crashes and injuries. Such programs are most successful when drivers are not forced to leave their vehicles at the drinking location: the best programs take the drinker to the drinking location and then return him to his home.

EVALUATING THE AUTHORS' ARGUMENTS:

The Center for Problem-Oriented Policing argues that a combination of drunk driving laws can reduce incidences of drunk driving. List the main reason why Mark R. Crovelli, author of the following viewpoint, would say this is incorrect.

Viewpoint

2

Stricter Laws Cannot Reduce Drunk Driving

Mark R. Crovelli

"It is naïve at best to think that the state's relatively mild form of punishment could possibly dissuade a man from driving drunk, when not even the risk of death was able to discourage him."

Mark R. Crovelli is a writer who lives in Denver, Colorado. In the following viewpoint he argues that strict drunk driving laws will not have any effect on drunk driving. This is because no law will ever come close to punishing a drunk driver as much as the natural consequences of his actions could. Crovelli says the worst consequences of drunk driving—death, serious injury, or killing or injuring others—exist with or without laws about drunk driving. He reasons that if drunk drivers are willing to drive drunk even though they know it might result in death, how could the threat of a stiff fine or lost license possibly dissuade them? Since no legal punishment for drunk driving will be worse than death, Crovelli concludes that drunk drivers are unable to be stopped by even the strictest of drunk driving laws.

The question of whether or not we ought to have draconian laws prohibiting drunk driving in this country hinges on another critical, yet all-too-often neglected question: Do drunk-driving laws actually reduce the incidence of drunk driving and thus make our roads and highways safer?

If we answer this question in the affirmative, and determine to our satisfaction that drunk-driving laws do actually reduce drunk driving and make our roads safer, then we might be justified in thinking that the laws are useful and protect the public. If, on the other hand, we determine that drunk-driving laws do not actually reduce the inci-dence of drunk driving or make our roads safer, then we would do well to ask ourselves whether we need these laws at all. What would be the use, after all, of fining, imprisoning and terrorizing American drivers, if this ruthless police action does not have the effect of mak-ing our roads safer places?

We Do Not Need Laws to Punish Drunk Driving

It is my contention in this article that drunk-driving laws do not actually reduce the incidence of drunk driving. Hence, it is absolutely absurd for the state to waste billions of dollars each year hunting down drunk-drivers, trying them in courts, fining them astronomi-cal amounts of money, and incarcerating them, when the state could effectively make America's roads and highways just as safe by loosen-ing up state licensing laws for taxi cabs and limousines.

In order for me to be able to make my case, I must first make some initial observations about drunk driving. First, it is important to note that when a man gets behind the wheel of an automobile while drunk he is taking a risk. His decision to drive drunk might result in him getting into a gruesome accident that takes his own life, the life of another driver, or other persons adjacent to him, or an accident that injures or seriously maims himself or other people. Should any of these scenarios actually occur, the drunk driver faces serious penalties—he could die in the accident, become permanently crippled or disfigured, or face charges for vehicular assault or murder if he hurts other people. These potential penalties for drunk driving

Stricter Laws Do Not Prevent Drunk Driving Deaths

The number of alcohol-related deaths remains constant from year to year. Some argue this is because laws against drunk driving have no effect on whether people will drive drunk.

Traffic Fatality Trends, 2000–2006

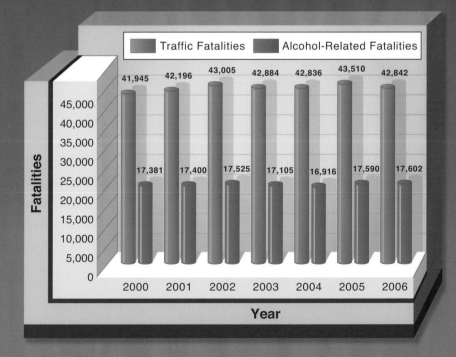

Taken from: National Highway Traffic Safety Administration, 2007.

exist *even in the absence of stiff drunk-driving laws enacted by the state.* In other words, even if there were no laws prohibiting drunk driving in this country, people who chose to drive drunk, *and caused serious injury to others*, would still face serious legal consequences for their actions—in addition to the possible injuries and death that they might cause themselves.

Drunk Driving Laws Cannot Be Effective

The case for ruthless laws punishing drunk driving rests on the assumption that these inherent and omnipresent penalties for drunk driving, (like death, disfigurement or a life sentence in prison), will not act as an effective deterrent. Drunk drivers, it is held, will discount the possibility of getting into a fiery crash that will kill them or send them to prison, (because of their "impaired judgment," to use the preferred nomenclature), which means that the state must step in and create additional penalties for drunk driving that will discourage the act even further. The state, then, swoops in with harsh penalties for driving while drunk or alcohol impaired, in the hope, (it is claimed, at least), of making our roads and highways safer by reducing the number of impaired drivers on the road. . . .

It all sounds so reasonable: because of their "impaired judgment," drunk drivers discount the danger of dying or hurting other people, so the state must implement harsh laws that discourage drunk driving even more. The problem with this idea, however, is that the state's penalties for drunk driving are extremely lenient when compared to what could possibly occur as a natural consequence of drunk driving—like, death, disfigurement or a lifetime in prison. As such, it is naïve at best to think that the state's relatively mild form of punishment could possibly dissuade a man from driving drunk, when not even the risk of death was able to discourage him from doing so.

> # FAST FACT
>
> National Highway Traffic Safety Administration statistics show that alcohol-related fatality figures have stayed about the same for the past decade—despite lowered blood-alcohol standards, the use of roadblocks and sobriety checkpoints, and other measures.

In other words, what the state and other logic-eschewing groups would like for us to believe is the following:

A. When a man is drunk, his "impaired judgment" makes him discount the possibility of getting into a horrible accident that might kill or injure him or someone else. As a result of discounting this risk, he is likely to go ahead and drive drunk anyway.
B. This same drunken man, who thinks he can cheat death on the highway, will suddenly see the light, shut off his engine, and walk home if the state merely threatens him with a stint in jail if he drives.

Drunk Drivers Are Not Deterred by Punishment

If we look at these propositions without letting emotion cloud our judgment, is it not obvious that if a man thinks he can drive home and avoid killing himself or hurting other people (because of his "impaired judgment"), *he is likely to think the very same thing about avoiding the relatively mild punishments of the police?* What could possibly make us think that threatening a man with a lighter punishment than could result as a natural consequence of his actions will dissuade him from doing something, when the threat of the more severe natural punishments does not? Is this not similar to what occurs when the police attempt to deter "base jumping" in national parks by threatening to fine those who jump? If a man thinks he can avoid the natural and severe potential punishment of jumping off a cliff, (i.e., squashing himself on the rocks thousands of feet below), what could possibly make us think that the threat of a $500 fine will stop him?

My argument can be summed up with the following proposition:

If a man is intoxicated to the extent that he is a danger to himself and other drivers, and he believes that he is capable of avoiding killing himself or injuring others on the road, then he is just as likely to believe that he can avoid getting caught by the police.

Increase Public Transit

It is true, I will concede, that the state's drunk-driving laws probably do dissuade a few people from driving with alcohol in their veins.

Eliminating cumbersome licensing laws for taxis and limousines could reduce the cost of sober transportation, making drunk drivers more likely to use the services.

Some people probably are dissuaded from driving home from a restaurant after consuming two or three glasses of wine, and some college students probably designate a driver so that they do not all have to drive home from the party drunk. Big deal. Dissuading these people from driving while drunk could be accomplished just as effectively and without creating a police state *by eliminating all licensing laws on taxi cabs and limousines in the United States, which would drastically reduce the cost and increase the supply of sober transportation for Americans.* If taxis and limousines were as cheap in the United States as they are in Mexico, for example, do you really think that Americans would choose to drive while intoxicated in the same numbers as they presently do? If mom and dad could take a cheap taxi to the restaurant and *both* drink three or four glasses of wine, *and* make it home safely, don't you think that they would choose to do so? Wouldn't they prefer this to having mom sit through another dinner *sans vin* [without wine] as the "designated driver," while dad inhales whiskey sours? And don't you think college students would prefer to catch a ride to the party safely in a cheap limousine—*with a bar inside*—than for all of them to drive separately and dangerously after drinking? Finally, don't you think that the serious alcoholic would prefer to catch a cheap and safe ride to his local tavern and back home safely, rather than waking up in county jail? That he doesn't do so already has something to do with the fact that to catch a ride in a taxi will likely cost him more than his bar tab will.

There is thus no need to waste billions of dollars hunting down people who have had a few glasses of wine with dinner, trying them in court, and then sentencing them to jail—especially when these laws will have no effect on those people who are truly dangerously intoxicated and who believe that they can both drive home safely *and* avoid getting caught by the police. As usual, the source of a serious social ill lies in the state's own laws and regulations, and the solution lies in the realm of the free-market.

EVALUATING THE AUTHOR'S ARGUMENTS:

At the heart of Crovelli's argument is the assumption that no legal punishment is steep enough to dissuade someone who is willing to risk his or her life, or the lives of others, by driving drunk. Do you think Crovelli is right? Why or why not? As a result, what do you think should be done about drunk driving laws?

Sobriety Checkpoints Reduce Drunk Driving

Danielle E. Roeber

"Sobriety checkpoints are a proven measure to reduce impaired driving crashes, injuries, and fatalities."

Sobriety checkpoints are an effective way to reduce drunk driving accidents, injuries, and fatalities, argues Danielle E. Roeber in the following viewpoint. She explains that sobriety checkpoints have been in use since 1984, and since then have helped catch thousands of drunk drivers. Sobriety checkpoints work because they remove the illusion that a drunk driver will not get caught, explains Roeber. Many drunk drivers think they can go undetected if they drive cautiously, but Roeber argues that stopping everyone on a road regardless of how they are driving works to shatter that illusion. Roeber concludes that sobriety checkpoints should be used by more states, and more frequently.

Roeber is deputy director of the Office of Safety Recommendations and Advocacy for the National Transportation Safety Board.

Danielle E. Roeber, "Testimony Before the Committee on Criminal Jurisprudence, Texas House of Representatives, on Senate Bill 298—Sobriety Checkpoints, Austin, Texas," NTSB.gov, May 6, 2009. Reproduced by permission.

AS YOU READ, CONSIDER THE FOLLOWING QUESTIONS:
1. What percent of highway deaths does the author say are alcohol related?
2. What do sobriety checkpoints "preclude impaired drivers from assuming," according to Roeber?
3. What effect did sobriety checkpoints have in Tennessee in the 1990s, according to Roeber?

T he Safety Board has recognized for many years that motor vehicle crashes are responsible for more deaths than crashes in all other transportation modes combined. More than 90 percent of all transportation related deaths each year result from highway crashes. Each year, about 40 percent of highway deaths nationwide are alcohol-related. The number of alcohol-related fatalities, over 17,000 in 2007, remains substantially higher than in 1999, when approximately 15,790 people died in alcohol-related crashes.

The emotional toll on families is staggering, but impaired driving also has a financial impact. According to calculations by the National Highway Traffic Safety Administration (NHTSA), the lifetime cost to society for each fatality is over $977,000; alcohol-related crashes cost society billions of dollars. While the affected individual covers some of these costs, overall, NHTSA estimates that those *not* directly involved in crashes pay for nearly three-quarters of all crash costs, primarily through insurance premiums, taxes, and travel delay. Clearly, much needs to be done to reduce this ongoing tragedy.

The Hard Core Drinking Driver

The Safety Board is particularly concerned with hard core drinking drivers, who are involved in about 54 percent of alcohol-related fatalities. The Board defines hard core drinking drivers as individuals who drive with a blood alcohol concentration (BAC) of 0.15 percent or greater, or who are arrested for driving while intoxicated within 10 years of a prior driving while impaired (DWI) arrest. From 1983 through 2007, more than 220,000 people died in crashes involving hard core drinking drivers. Most experts agree that impaired drivers persist in their behavior because these drivers believe that they will

States That Allow Sobriety Checkpoints

The majority of states—38, plus the District of Columbia—use sobriety checkpoints to curb and catch drunk drivers.

States that conduct sobriety checkpoints

States that do not conduct sobriety checkpoints

Taken from: Insurance Institute for Highway Safety (IIHS) and State Highway Safety Offices, August 2009.

not be caught and/or convicted. That perception is based on reality. NHTSA estimates that on average, an individual makes about 1,000 drinking driving trips before being arrested.

In 1984, the Safety Board completed a safety study that included recommendations to reduce the problem of repeat DWI offenders. Since those recommendations were issued, all States have made efforts to address the alcohol-related highway safety problem, making considerable progress in detecting, arresting, and adjudicating drinking drivers. However, the measures taken and the degree of implementation of the Safety Board's 1984 recommendations by States and localities have not been uniform, and alcohol-related crashes continue to claim thousands of lives.

In light of the thousands of deaths still resulting from these crashes, the Safety Board focused on hard core drinking drivers in 2000. In that report, the Board examined a variety of countermeasures used by the States to identify which of these actions have been effective, and recommended a model program . . . to reduce hard core drinking driving. The problem of hard core drinking drivers is complex; no single countermeasure by itself appears to reduce recidivism and crashes sufficiently. We need a comprehensive system of prevention, apprehension, sanction, and treatment to reduce the crashes, injuries, and fatalities caused by these drivers.

Sobriety Checkpoints Work

Sobriety checkpoints have long been recognized as a key component of an effective impaired driving enforcement program. Indeed, the Safety Board first recommended that Texas and other States institute the use of sobriety checkpoints more than 20 years ago, in 1984.

Many DWI offenders persist in their behavior because their perception of being arrested and penalized is low. Focusing principally on those relatively few DWI offenders who have already been apprehended will not likely achieve significant reductions in impaired driving and alcohol-related crashes. States must take measures to convince motorists that there is a strong likelihood that they will be caught, thereby deterring impaired driving before an arrest.

> **FAST FACT**
>
> According to the Centers for Disease Control and Prevention, sobriety checkpoints reduce alcohol-related crashes by about 20 percent.

You Will Get Caught

Well publicized sobriety checkpoints are a key component of deterrence because they increase the perception among drivers who potentially would drive impaired that they will be caught. Since every

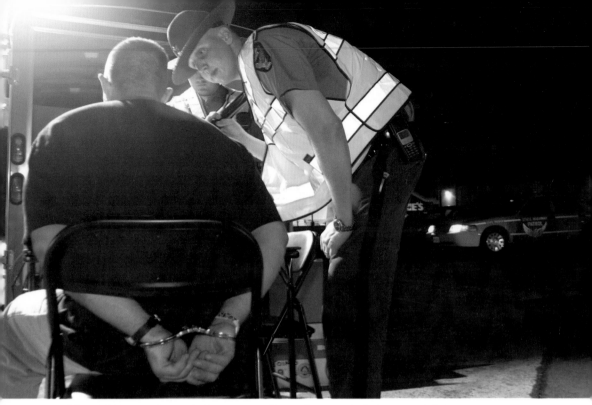

The author says sobriety checkpoints are effective because alcohol-impaired drivers cannot avoid detection by driving cautiously.

motorist is potentially subject to being stopped, sobriety checkpoints preclude impaired drivers from assuming that they can avoid detection merely by driving cautiously. Sobriety checkpoints also afford police the opportunity to contact greater numbers of motorists than during typical patrols, and demonstrate their jurisdiction's commitment to reducing drunk driving.

The effectiveness of sobriety checkpoints was documented in Tennessee's "Checkpoint Tennessee" program of the 1990's. Localities throughout Tennessee conducted sobriety checkpoints for a year. These were accompanied by extensive television, radio and print media coverage, both before and after the checkpoints. A subsequent analysis of the effects of the program on traffic deaths revealed a 20.4 percent reduction over the projected number of impaired driving fatal crashes that would have occurred without the checkpoint program. That translated into a reduction of 9 fatal crashes each month in Tennessee. The effect was still present 21 months later. Further, public opinion surveys conducted throughout the project indicated that over 90 percent of drivers supported the program.

Let Sobriety Checkpoints Work

Some have questioned the constitutionality of sobriety checkpoints. However, the Supreme Court of the United States upheld their use in 1990 (*Michigan Department of State Police v. Sitz*), on the grounds that preventing alcohol related crashes and deaths outweighs the "slight" intrusion on drivers who are stopped. The Supreme Court rejected arguments that checkpoints are a violation of the 4th Amendment.

Sobriety checkpoints are in widespread use throughout the nation. Currently, 38 States and the District of Columbia authorize the use of sobriety checkpoints. Senate Bill 298 will authorize, but not mandate, local police departments to use this very effective impaired driving countermeasure.

In 2006, almost 48 percent of highway fatalities in Texas involved alcohol, and more than 54 percent of alcohol-related fatalities involved a hard core drinking driver. Sobriety checkpoints are a proven measure to reduce impaired driving crashes, injuries, and fatalities. Sobriety checkpoints played a major role in reducing alcohol-related fatalities from over 28,000 per year in 1980 to about 17,000 in 2007. Texas needs to authorize, support, and regularly use sobriety checkpoints with the other measures included in the Safety Board's model program. As evidence of the importance of sobriety checkpoints and the other model program elements, the Board has placed the hard core drinking driving recommendation on its "Most Wanted" list of safety recommendations.

EVALUATING THE AUTHOR'S ARGUMENTS:

The author of this viewpoint works for the National Transportation Safety Board, a government agency responsible for investigating car, bus, plane, and other transportation accidents. Does knowing the background of this author influence your opinion of her argument? In what way?

Viewpoint

4

Sobriety Checkpoints Do Not Reduce Drunk Driving

Ken Krall

"I'm not sure that handing the remaining part of our privacy keys over is something we want to do as citizens."

In the following viewpoint Ken Krall argues that sobriety checkpoints are an invasion of privacy. He says the majority of people stopped by a checkpoint are not drunk but just regular citizens with places to go. He tells the story of being stopped at a checkpoint while trying to take his sick daughter to a doctor. The delay was worrisome considering his daughter's health, and he resented having to give confidential information to a police officer. Krall says that sobriety checkpoints infringe on the privacy of upstanding citizens and do little to curb drunk driving, since most drunk drivers avoid roads that they know to have checkpoints on them. He concludes that other methods can be used to curb drunk driving that do not threaten an important civil liberty.

Krall is a columnist for NewsoftheNorth .Net, Inc., an online news site in Wisconsin, where this viewpoint was originally published.

The Wisconsin legislature will soon be looking at strengthening the state's drunk driving laws. Unless you keep track of such things, you might not know we have the nation's most lenient drunk driving laws.

Without a full recitation of it, compared to 49 other states, in Wisconsin you catch a break the first time you're arrested and you also catch a break a few other times, until you eventually get locked up (or get into treatment which should have occurred long before).

Law enforcement has done a credible job using current techniques, and the number of alcohol-related fatalities is going down. Injuries caused by people drinking and driving are always a concern, as drunk driving, like smoking, is wholly preventable.

While some might say they have been plenty penalized after the first Driving While Intoxicated (fines, license suspension and a whopping increase in car insurance costs), we still catch a break here compared to other states, where the first offense is a felony.

What I'm going to talk about next is not a defense of drunk driving. There is no defense for drunk, buzzed or impaired driving of any kind, including driving on ice with one hand on the wheel and the other on your cell phone.

Sobriety Checkpoints Threaten Privacy

But one or the proposals being pushed by well-intentioned people calls for the use of sobriety checkpoints to "get the drunks off the road." While I go along with the other proposals, I want to ask people to consider whether sobriety checkpoints might be going too far.

In case you don't know, what happens is you are required, regardless of circumstance, to stop your vehicle while law enforcement checks you out. These checkpoints can be extremely effective, at first (until the word gets out and the drunks drive on other roads). That isn't the issue. What I question is whether you as a driver forfeit all your rights to privacy by simply going on the road?

Sober as a judge, you might be driving at 2 a.m. on a Sunday morning. Ahead is a notice that you must pull over into the checkpoint with the force of law enforcement behind it. Up comes a deputy, flashlight in hand, to check out your license and condition. Of course you've done nothing wrong, but after checking out your credentials, etc., you are waved through.

Supporters would say, "So what? If you haven't done anything wrong there's nothing to worry about." There's a grain of truth there, but it also was some of the logic used by the [George W.] Bush Administration to support the nearly single-largest stripping of our individual rights, called the "Patriot" Act. If you aren't doing anything *we* disagree with, you don't have anything to worry about, or so it goes with that piece of very flawed legislation.

Ordinary Citizens Are Harassed

Let me give you a personal history here. I was transporting my then three-year-old daughter in the late '80s to a doctor's appointment and was heading down Hwy. 97 to the Marshfield Clinic about 10 a.m. Partly cloudy, warm-weather day, dry roads.

Ahead I was told I had to stop at a Department of Transportation [DOT] checkpoint. Smack-dab in the traffic lane the DOT had blocked off the road, leaving a lane for the cars to queue into. As a background, up to that day, the doctors at Marshfield thought it was possible my daughter was very ill. My daughter didn't know how potentially sick she was, and my wife and I were worried sick.

I drove up to the "stop" point, where a DOT technocrat began asking me (after they had checked my license plate), "Where are you from?", "Where are you going?", "What is the nature of your trip?" The last one set me off. As a "free" citizen of the U.S., no bureaucrat needed to know what I was doing that day, no way, no how.

But rather than explode at the technocrat (there was a State Patrol car nearby) I answered the questions and took off. On the following Monday, I called then-State Sen. Lloyd Kincaid to complain. I told him we were late for a doctor's appointment because I was pulled over and grilled by the DOT, wanting to know more personal information than I wanted to divulge. He took my call and checked it out with the DOT. He called me back and said he was unaware the state was doing the checkpoints and he had straightened it out with them, and apologized for having put me through it.

Going Too Far to Solve a Problem

I never saw another checkpoint. I'm sure to some bureaucrat this was valuable information for their purposes, but somewhere someone forgot that that information could be used by anyone with access to

Critics say sobriety checkpoints infringe upon the rights of innocent citizens while drunks simply avoid them.

How Well Do Sobriety Checkpoints Work?

Opponents of sobriety checkpoints say they do not reduce drunk driving fatalities and accidents because drunk drivers can too easily find out where the checkpoints are and avoid them. In Oregon, for example, alcohol-related fatalities have continued to fall even since sobriety checkpoints were outlawed in 1987. This proves, say opponents, that sobriety checkpoints have no effect on drunk driving.

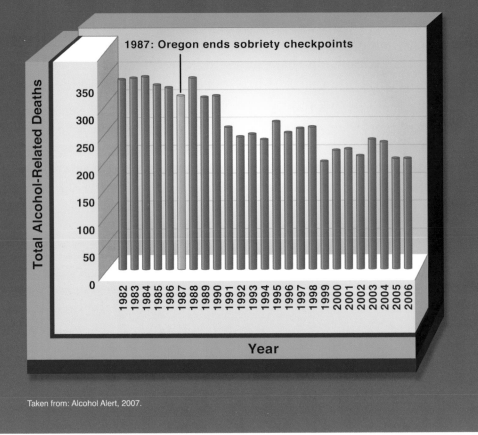

Taken from: Alcohol Alert, 2007.

your files. Do you believe it when people say stuff is confidential? I don't.

As it turned out, our daughter's condition was not as serious as first thought and she recovered, but I never recovered from being pulled over, fully sober but deathly worried, while some creep was grilling me with a police car nearby. I had nothing to worry about, did I, but is this right?

Supporters of sobriety checkpoints are often the living victims of the senseless impacts of drunk driving. Their trauma can never be taken away, and bless all of them. But as citizens we also have to ask whether we should simply give over all our rights to stop a problem. In some countries they cut off the hand of a thief. It's effective, so why don't we do it here? Perhaps we see it as going too far to correct the problem.

Wisconsin is an "Implied Consent" state, which means law enforcement has the right to take some liberties with you *with just cause* to see if you can safely operate a vehicle. Being a law enforcement officer is a tough job and stopping drunks is just one part of it. They do a remarkably good job of it given current tools.

I'm not sure that handing the remaining part of our privacy keys over is something we want to do as citizens. Strengthening current laws, like requiring jail time for the first offense, might reduce the repeat offenders. Remember, the government is supposed to work for us, not the other way around.

To those of you who think I'm supporting drunk driving, please re-read my second paragraph, and don't drink and drive.

EVALUATING THE AUTHORS' ARGUMENTS:

Ken Krall suggests that personal liberty and privacy are more important than catching a few drunk drivers. What do you think? Write one or two sentences on whether you think he is right. Then, write one or two sentences on what each of the other authors in this chapter would say about this argument.

Ignition Interlock Devices Reduce Drunk Driving

PR Newswire

"Ignition interlocks are proven to be an effective tool in the battle against drunk driving."

PR Newswire gives background on a bill that was passed in the Virginia House of Delegates that requires ignition interlock devices to be installed on vehicles of all first-time drunk driving offenders. The bill focuses on first-time offenders because research shows that these offenders have already driven under the influence many times prior to their first conviction. The bill promotes the use of the advanced technology tool of ignition interlock devices (IIDs), which have proven very effective when used properly. A driver must breathe into the device, which is connected to the vehicle's ignition system. The device then measures the blood alcohol content (BAC), and, if the BAC is higher than the set limit, the car will not start.

PR Newswire is a news service hired by corporations, public relations firms, and nongovernmental organizations to deliver news and multimedia content.

AS YOU READ, CONSIDER THE FOLLOWING QUESTIONS:
  1. What percentage of drunk drivers continue to drive, even when their licenses have been suspended?
  2. How effective are ignition interlock devices at preventing first-time and repeat offenders from recommitting the crime, as long as the device is installed on the vehicle?
  3. What percentage of drunk driving offenders believe that IIDs are effective and fair?

National leaders from Mothers Against Drunk Driving (MADD), Virginia Del. Sal Iaquinto, R-Virginia Beach, and others affected by drunk drivers today urged the state Senate to pass H.B. 1442, a bill that would require alcohol ignition interlocks to be installed on the vehicles of all first-time drunk driving offenders in Virginia. The measure overwhelmingly was approved by the House of Delegates on Tuesday by an 80-18 vote.

"Our vision of eliminating drunk driving can become a reality," said Glynn Birch, National President of MADD. "The first step is implementing proven solutions that currently exist to prevent deaths and injuries due to drunk driving. One solution is alcohol ignition interlocks, which could not only save thousands of lives, but also gives offenders the ability to drive without endangering the public." An alcohol ignition interlock is a breath test device linked to a vehicle's ignition system. Interlocks are used as a condition of probation for drunk driving offenders after their driver's licenses have been reinstated. When a driver wishes to start his or her vehicle, he or she must first blow into the device, but the vehicle will not start unless the driver's alcohol level is below the illegal limit of .08.

While interlocks are proven to save lives, it is estimated that only one out of eight convicted drunk drivers each year currently has an

> **FAST FACT**
>
> According to Mothers Against Drunk Driving, ignition interlock devices reduce drunk driving offenses by an average of 64 percent.

Most States Use Ignition Interlock Devices

Just a handful of states do not use ignition interlock devices to reduce the number of drivers who will drive drunk again.

States that use ignition interlock devices

States that do not use ignition interlock devices

Taken from: Mothers Against Drunk Driving, 2007. www.madd.org.

interlock on their vehicle. Currently, Virginia drunk driving laws only require ignition interlocks for those convicted of a second or subsequent drunk driving offense or those found to have a BAC at or above .15. Because these laws do not require first-time offenders to have an interlock, Virginians are sharing the road with thousands of convicted drunk drivers each time they back out of their driveway.

Research shows that first-time offenders arrested for drunk driving have driven drunk more than 87 times before their first arrest. In addition, studies estimate that 50 to 75 percent of drunk drivers whose licenses are suspended continue to drive. While this bill would ensure that Virginia's roadways are safer by preventing drunk drivers from committing the crime again, the maintenance and installation costs related to these devices would be covered by the offender, not Virginia taxpayers.

"The only way to ensure that convicted drunk drivers stop harming people is to make sure that they do not drink and drive again," said Del. Iaquinto, "This bill does that—and will make the Commonwealth's roadways safer for all Virginia families."

Fortunately for Virginia and the rest of the nation, alcohol ignition interlocks are proven to be an effective tool in the battle against drunk driving. Studies have shown alcohol ignition interlocks are up to 90 percent effective in keeping both first-time and repeat offenders from recommitting the crime, as long as the interlock is installed on the vehicle. Because of their effectiveness, the devices have the potential to save more than 4,000 lives now lost in repeat drunk driving crashes annually. And the public has noticed, as 85 percent approve the use of interlocks for repeat offenders and 65 percent approve their installation in the vehicles of first-time offenders. Even 82 percent of offenders believe that interlocks are effective and fair.

Ignition-locking devices require drivers to blow into a tube to test their sobriety in order to start their car.

"We know that the technology works," says Chuck Hurley, CEO of MADD. "Now we need to implement these advances on our roads, every day in every state across the nation. Too many drunk driving offenders are back on the road, and it is our duty to ensure that they do not risk the lives of others and that they only drive while sober."

MADD believes the tools are now at hand to eliminate drunk driving from the United States. The Campaign to Eliminate Drunk Driving, launched in November 2006, has four elements: intensive, high-visibility law enforcement, full implementation of alcohol ignition interlocks for all convicted drunk drivers, development of advanced vehicle technologies to prevent drunk driving and grassroots support led by MADD and its 400+ affiliates, to make the elimination of drunk driving a reality.

"The real possibility of eliminating drunk driving in this country is a powerful, even audacious, idea. Yet the tools are now at hand. Using advanced technology, tougher enforcement, stronger laws and grassroots mobilization, the goal of eliminating a primary public health threat that has plagued the United States is within our reach," said Birch, whose 21-month-old son was killed by a drunk driver in 1988.

MADD's mission is to stop drunk driving, support the victims of this violent crime and prevent underage drinking. MADD is a 501 (c) (3) charity with 2 million members and supporters nationwide. Founded in 1980, MADD has helped save more than 330,000 lives. For more information, visit http://www.madd.org/.

EVALUATING THE AUTHORS' ARGUMENTS:

In this viewpoint, PR Newswire provides information that supports the use of ignition interlock devices. Compare this view with the next viewpoint by Charles Peña, who argues against universal use of ignition interlock devices on all vehicles. What bias, if any, is represented in each viewpoint? What common ground is there, and at what point do views begin to shift from that common ground? Support your answer with evidence from each viewpoint.

Ignition Interlock Devices Should Not Be Widely Used

Charles Peña

"Requiring the rest of the driving public to pass the same test [as hard-core drunk drivers] makes us a society of suspects and violates the fundamental principle of presumed innocence."

Ignition interlock devices (IIDs) are not a cure-all for drunk driving, Charles Peña argues in the following viewpoint. He thinks they are effective at stopping a hard-core drunk driver from driving drunk in the future but is against installing them on all vehicles. Peña imagines a scenario in which a responsible drinker has a glass of wine with dinner and then needs to use her car for an emergency. An ignition interlock device would prevent her from driving, even though she would not be impaired after just one drink. Peña also says that IIDs are prone to giving false positives, and as a result, hundreds of thousands of sober people would be locked out of their cars each day, unable to get to work or pick their kids up from school. For all these reasons, Peña concludes that

Charles Peña, "Ignition Interlock Is Not a Panacea," The Independent Institute, December 1, 2008. Reproduced by permission of The Independent Institute, 100 Swan Way, Oakland, CA 94021-1428 USA. http://www.independent.org/newsroom/article.asp?id=231.

IIDs should be used sparingly and not as a widespread response to the problem of drunk driving.

Peña is a senior fellow at both the Independent Institute and the Coalition for a Realistic Foreign Policy.

AS YOU READ, CONSIDER THE FOLLOWING QUESTIONS:
1. What does Peña say is the legal limit for blood alcohol content? What level would mandatory ignition interlock devices be set to detect?
2. How many sober people does Peña guess could be locked out of their cars each day as a result of IID error?
3. To make his argument, Peña quotes Mark Twain. What is the quote? What does it mean in the context of the viewpoint?

Technology has allowed cars to be safer—anti-lock brakes to prevent lock-up and skidding, air bags to provide protection in a crash and Bluetooth to allow hands-free phone calls are just a few examples. The first two are pretty much standard equipment nowadays, and the latter is becoming more widespread.

But some automobile manufacturers are considering adding another option in the name of safety: an ignition interlock, or alcohol sensor, to prevent someone from driving while drunk.

Ignition Interlock Devices Are Not Right for Everyone

On the surface, this seems like a reasonable enough idea. After all, no one is in favor of drunken driving, which resulted in nearly 13,000 traffic deaths in 2007 (a favorable 38% decrease since 1982). But should such devices be ubiquitous and should everyone—regardless of their driving history—be forced to pass an alcohol test to be able to drive their car?

Some safety advocates, such as the Governors Highway Safety Association, Mothers Against Drunk Driving and several states (New Mexico, New York, Pennsylvania and Oklahoma) seem to think more universal application would be a good idea.

Certainly, ignition interlock devices make sense for the most dangerous drunken drivers—those with high blood-alcohol content (the legal limit is 0.08 BAC, and the average BAC for a drunken driver involved in a fatal crash is more than twice that), who also happen to most likely be repeat offenders. But requiring the rest of the driving public to pass the same test makes us a society of suspects and violates the fundamental principle of presumed innocence.

IIDs Would Prevent Sober People from Using Their Cars

Furthermore and more troubling, once this technology—which has advanced to include passive mechanisms like steering wheel sensors,

"Idiot Driver Sensor System," cartoon by Betsy Streeter. www.CartoonStock.com. Copyright © Betsy Streeter. Reproduction rights obtainable from www.CartoonStock.com.

retinal scans and alcohol sniffers—comes as standard equipment in all cars, it will be set well below the legal limit of 0.08.

Twenty-four states have what is known as "presumptive intoxication levels," which means that a driver can be arrested and convicted of DUI [driving under the influence] at levels as low as 0.04 and 0.05 BAC. In all states, mandatory interlocks would be set below those levels, due to product liability concerns and variances in technology. Interlocks in all cars set at such low levels would effectively eliminate the ability to drive after having only one drink for many adults.

Imagine if you were home having a glass of wine with dinner and you get a call that one of your children is hurt or sick and in an emergency situation. Imagine not being able to get to them because your car decided that the wine you just drank was enough to lock you out of driving. That's not an anti–drunken driving safety device; that's a neo-Prohibitionist enforcement device—evidence that groups such as MADD have strayed from their original purpose to combat drunken driving.

IIDs Are Prone to Error

There is also a practical aspect to making ignition interlock mandatory on all cars. Let's assume that ignition interlock technology is nearly perfect—99.99% accurate (which is generous and highly unlikely) in correctly measuring BAC. If half of all the licensed drivers (120 million people) drive to and from work each day, the number of false positives—i.e., people incorrectly identified as exceeding the set BAC limit—would be 12,000 each time those people tried to start their cars. So 24,000 times a day, drivers who simply are trying to drive to work or pick up their children from school each day would be prevented from driving their cars because they were erroneously identified as drunk.

Because some states set "presumptive intoxication levels" below the legal limits for driving under the influence, critics say ignition-locking devices must be set at an even lower level. This could prevent a legally sober person from driving.

Too Harsh a Punishment

If not everyone, then why not mandate ignition interlocks for everyone convicted of drunken driving? Because an important principle of jurisprudence is that the punishment should fit the crime. Someone exceeding the speed limit by 25 mph (usually considered reckless driving) receives a different punishment than someone who is only 5 mph over the posted speed limit.

So someone—especially a first-time offender—at the legal limit of 0.08 BAC should not automatically receive the same punishment as someone driving at more than twice that and with prior convictions. For the former (and it's worth noting for perspective that various studies indicate driving while talking on a cell phone is more dangerous than driving at 0.08 BAC), the court should have the discretion to determine the appropriate punishment. This would not preclude an ignition interlock if circumstances warranted.

One of many of Mark Twain's memorable phrases is: "To a man with a hammer, everything looks like a nail." Ultimately, that is the problem with the ignition interlock proponents. It can be an effective device to use with high BAC and habitual drunken drivers. But it's a solution in search of a problem for the rest of society.

EVALUATING THE AUTHOR'S ARGUMENTS:

Peña suggests that people who want to make ignition interlock devices a routine safety device on all vehicles do not really want to reduce drunk driving as much as they want to curb the public's enjoyment of certain freedoms, such as responsibly drinking alcohol. Do you agree with him? Why or why not? In your answer, use evidence from the texts you have read.

Facts About Alcohol

Editor's note: These facts can be used in reports or papers to reinforce or add credibility when making important points or claims.

Facts About Binge Drinking and Underage Drinking

According to the Centers for Disease Control and Prevention:

- Excessive alcohol consumption contributes to more than forty-six hundred deaths among underage Americans each year.
- Underage drinking is linked with alcohol-impaired driving, physical fighting, poor school performance, sexual activity, and smoking.
- Binge drinking by adults is a strong predictor of binge drinking by college students living in the same state.
- Approximately 1.5 billion episodes of binge drinking occur among persons aged eighteen years or older in the United States annually.
- More than 90 percent of adult binge drinkers are not alcohol dependent.
- Maintaining a minimum legal drinking age of twenty-one would prevent a 16 percent increase in motor vehicle crashes among underage youth.
- States with more stringent alcohol control policies tend to have lower adult and college binge drinking rates.

According to Mothers Against Drunk Driving:

- In 2006 about 10.8 million young people aged twelve to twenty (28.3 percent) reported drinking alcohol in the past month.
- Approximately 7.2 million (19.0 percent) were binge drinkers; 2.4 million (6.2 percent) were heavy drinkers.
- Alcohol is the number one drug problem among American youth.
- More young people die from alcohol-related incidents than from all other accidents involving illicit drugs combined.

- Parents are the most common suppliers of alcohol to people under age twenty-one.
- Underage drinking costs American taxpayers approximately $61.9 billion each year.
- Those who start drinking before age fifteen are twelve times more likely to be unintentionally injured while under the influence of alcohol, seven times more likely to be in a car accident, and ten times more likely to get into a fight.
- Youth who have their first drink before age thirteen are twice as likely to have unplanned sex and more than twice as likely to have unprotected sex.

Facts About the Drinking Age

Alcohol was prohibited in the United States between 1919 and 1933. When it became legal again in 1933, states were free to regulate alcohol as they wanted.

After 1933, thirty-two states adopted a minimum legal drinking age of twenty-one, and sixteen chose a minimum legal drinking age of from eighteen to twenty.

Between 1970 and 1976, thirty states lowered their minimum legal drinking age from twenty-one to eighteen. These changes took place as other rights were being granted to young people, such as the right of eighteen-year-olds to vote.

In 1984 the National Minimum Drinking Age Act required all states to raise the age that people were allowed to buy and possess alcohol to twenty-one. States that did not comply became ineligible to receive federal highway funding.

According to the State University of New York, Potsdam:

- The United States is one of four countries that has a drinking age of twenty-one. The other three are Fiji, Palau, and Sri Lanka. Pakistan allows non-Muslims to drink when they are twenty-one, but alcohol is prohibited for Muslims.

- In twelve countries, the drinking age is sixteen.
- In one country, the drinking age is seventeen.
- In eighty-two countries, the drinking age is eighteen.
- In two countries, the drinking age is nineteen.
- In three countries, the drinking age is twenty.
- Seventeen countries have no minimum drinking age.

The National Highway Traffic Safety Administration (NHTSA) estimates that the over-twenty-one drinking age saves only about 923 lives per year, compared with:

- seatbelts (estimated to save 15,434 lives per year),
- airbags (2,647 lives per year),
- motorcycle helmets (1,316 lives per year), and
- child restraints (451 lives per year).

According to researchers at the University of Georgia who studied alcohol-related incidents in the 1970s and early 1980s when the drinking age was eighteen, a lowered drinking age increases:

- prenatal alcohol consumption among eighteen- to twenty-year-old women by 21 percent;
- the number of births to eighteen- to twenty-year-olds by 4.6 percent in white women and 3.9 percent in eighteen- to twenty-year-old African American women;
- the likelihood of women under age twenty-one having a low-birth-weight baby by 6 percent (4 percent for white women and 8 percent for African American women);
- the likelihood of premature birth by 5 percent in white women under age eighteen and by 7 percent in African American women under age eighteen;
- the probability of an unplanned pregnancy by 25 percent for African American women

According to Mothers Against Drunk Driving:

- By the end of 2009, the twenty-one minimum drinking age law had saved nearly twenty-nine thousand American lives.
- Since the twenty-one minimum drinking age was adopted in the 1980s, the number of young people killed annually in crashes involving drunk drivers under twenty-one has been cut in half.

According to a July 2007 Gallup poll:

- 77 percent of Americans say they would oppose a federal law that would lower the drinking age in all states to eighteen.
- 60 percent support stricter penalties for underage drinking.

Facts About Drunk Driving

According to Mothers Against Drunk Driving:

- only one arrest is made for every eighty-eight episodes of driving over the illegal limit.
- traffic crashes are the number one killer of teens, and 28 percent of fatal traffic crashes involving teen drivers are alcohol-related.

According to the California Highway Patrol:

- 50 percent of Americans will be involved in an alcohol-involved traffic collision in his or her lifetime.
- Nearly twenty-three thousand people are killed every year in alcohol-related traffic collisions.
- One American life is lost every twenty-two minutes in an alcohol-related traffic collision.

According to the National Highway Transportation Safety Administration:

Alcohol-related fatalities went down 9.7 percent from 2007 to 2008, from 13,041 deaths to 11,773.

In 2008 alcohol-related traffic deaths accounted for 32 percent of all traffic fatalities.

Alcohol accounts for a significant percentage of all traffic fatalities in all fifty states and the District of Columbia. Nebraska has the highest rate of alcohol-related traffic deaths:

- Alabama—34%
- Alaska—30%
- Arizona—32%
- Arkansas—28%
- California—28%
- Colorado—30%
- Connecticut—37%
- Delaware—41%
- District of Columbia—37%
- Florida—29%

- Georgia—27%
- Idaho—28%
- Indiana—25%
- Kansas—26%
- Louisiana—38%
- Maryland—29%
- Michigan—28%
- Mississippi—36%
- Montana—38%
- Nevada—32%
- New Jersey—28%
- New York—28%
- North Dakota—48%
- Oklahoma—29%
- Pennsylvania—34%
- South Carolina—43%
- Tennessee—31%
- Utah—19%
- Virginia—29%
- West Virginia—32%
- Wyoming—33%
- Hawaii—32%
- Illinois—35%
- Iowa—24%
- Kentucky—25%
- Maine—36%
- Massachusetts—36%
- Minnesota—34%
- Missouri—34%
- Nebraska—30%
- New Hampshire—26%
- New Mexico—32%
- North Carolina—30%
- Ohio—31%
- Oregon—33%
- Rhode Island—32%
- South Dakota—30%
- Texas—38%
- Vermont—34%
- Washington—34%
- Wisconsin—42%

Facts About Sobriety Checkpoints

According to the Centers for Disease Control and Prevention, sobriety checkpoints reduce alcohol-related crashes and fatalities by 18 to 24 percent.

According to Mothers Against Drunk Driving, 70 to 80 percent of the public supports the use of sobriety checkpoints.

Organizations to Contact

The editors have compiled the following list of organizations concerned with the issues debated in this book. The descriptions are derived from materials provided by the organizations. All have publications or information available for interested readers. The list was compiled on the date of publication of the present volume; the information provided here may change. Be aware that many organizations take several weeks or longer to respond to inquiries, so allow as much time as possible for the receipt of requested materials.

Advocates for Highway and Auto Safety
750 First St. NE, Ste. 901
Washington, DC 2002
(202) 408-1711
fax: (202) 408-1699
e-mail: advocates@saferoads.org
Web site: www.saferoads.org

An alliance of consumer, health, and safety groups and insurance companies, this organization encourages adoption of laws, policies, and programs that save lives and reduce injuries. The group's Web site has information and news on a variety of highway safety issues, including drunk driving and teen driving.

Al-Anon Family Group Headquarters
1600 Corporate Landing Pkwy.
Virginia Beach, VA 23454
(757) 563-1600
Web site: www.al-anon.alateen.org

Al-Anon is a fellowship of men, women, and children whose lives have been affected by an alcoholic family member or friend. Members share their experiences, strength, and hope to help each other and perhaps to aid in the recovery of the alcoholic. Al-Anon Family Group Headquarters provides information on its local chapters and on its affiliated organization, Alateen.

Alcoholics Anonymous (AA)
PO Box 459
New York, NY 10163
(212) 870-3400
Web site: www.aa.org

Alcoholics Anonymous is an international fellowship of people who are recovering from alcoholism. Because AA's primary goal is to help alcoholics remain sober, it does not sponsor research or engage in education about alcoholism. AA does, however, publish a catalog of literature concerning the organization as well as several pamphlets, including *Is AA for You? Young People and AA*, and *A Brief Guide to Alcoholics Anonymous*.

American Beverage Institute (ABI)
1090 Vermont Ave. NW, Ste. 800
Washington, DC 20005
(202) 463-7110
Web site: www.abionline.org

The American Beverage Institute is a restaurant industry trade organization that works to protect the consumption of alcoholic beverages in the restaurant setting. It unites the wine, beer, and spirits producers with distributors and on-premise retailers in this effort. It conducts research and education in an attempt to demonstrate that the vast majority of adults who drink alcohol outside of the home are responsible, law-abiding citizens. Its Web site includes fact sheets and news articles on various issues, such as drunk driving laws and alcohol taxes.

American Society of Addiction Medicine (ASAM)
4601 N. Park Ave., Upper Arcade #101
Chevy Chase, MD 20815
(301) 656-3920
e-mail: email@asam.org
Web site: www.asam.org

ASAM is the nation's addiction medicine specialty society dedicated to educating physicians and improving the treatment of individuals suffering from alcoholism and other addictions. In addition, the organization promotes research and prevention of addiction and works for the establishment of addiction medicine as a specialty recognized by the American Board of Medical Specialties. The organization publishes medical texts and a bimonthly newsletter.

The Beer Institute
122 C St. NW, Ste. 750
Washington, DC 20001
(202) 737-2337
e-mail: info@beerinstitute.org
Web site: www.beerinstitute.org

The Beer Institute is a trade organization that represents the beer industry before Congress, state legislatures, and public forums across the country. It sponsors educational programs to prevent underage drinking and drunk driving and distributes fact sheets and news briefs on issues such as alcohol taxes and advertising. Its *Beer Institute Bulletin* newsletter is published four times a year.

Campaign Against Drunk Driving (CADD)
PO Box 62
Brighouse, West Yorkshire HD6 3YY
+44 (0) 845-123-5541
e-mail: cadd@scard.org.uk
Web site: www.cadd.org.uk

This British organization is dedicated to providing support to victims of drunk driving and to promoting stronger drunk driving laws, including a lower BAC level. Its Web site provides sources for drunk driving statistics in Great Britain.

Canadian Centre on Substance Abuse (CCSA/CLAT)
75 Albert St., Ste. 300
Ottawa, ON K1P 5E7, Canada
(613) 235-4048
Web site: www.ccsa.ca

A Canadian clearinghouse on substance abuse, this organization works to disseminate information on the nature, extent, and consequences of substance abuse and to support and assist organizations involved in substance abuse treatment, prevention, and educational programming. The CCSA/CCLAT publishes several books, reports, policy documents, brochures, research papers, and newsletters related to alcohol abuse.

Center for Science in the Public Interest (CSPI)
1875 Connecticut Ave. NW, Ste. 300
Washington, DC 20009
(202) 332-9110
e-mail: cspi@cspinet.org
Web site: www.cspinet.org

The center is an advocacy organization that promotes nutrition and health, food safety, alcohol policy, and sound science. It favors the implementation of public policies aimed at reducing alcohol-related problems, such as restricting alcohol advertising, increasing alcohol taxes, and reducing drunk driving.

The Century Council
2345 Crystal Dr., Ste. 910
Arlington, VA 22202
(202) 637-0077
Web site: www.centurycouncil.org

A nonprofit organization funded by America's liquor industry, the Century Council's mission is to fight drunk driving and underage drinking. It promotes responsible decision making about drinking and discourages all forms of irresponsible alcohol consumption through education, communications, research, law enforcement, and other programs. The Web site offers fact sheets and other resources on drunk driving, underage drinking, and other alcohol-related problems.

Distilled Spirits Council of the United States (DISCUS)
1250 Eye St. NW, Ste. 900
Washington, DC 20005
(202) 628-3544
Web site: www.discus.org

The Distilled Spirits Council of the United States is the national trade association representing producers and marketers of distilled spirits in the United States. It seeks to ensure the responsible advertising and marketing of distilled spirits to adult consumers and to prevent such advertising and marketing from targeting individuals below the legal purchase age. DISCUS publishes fact sheets, news releases, and other documents.

DWI Resource Center, Inc.
PO Box 30514
Albuquerque, NM 87190
(888) 410-1084
Web site: http://dwiresourcecenter.org
e-mail: info@dwiresourcecenter.org

This organization is dedicated to reducing the number of alcohol-related traffic fatalities through education, public awareness, prevention, and research. It serves as a central clearinghouse of DWI information and issues, providing community leaders with statistical information and analysis to assist them in creating localized plans to reduce DWI death and injury.

Insurance Institute for Highway Safety (IIHS)
1005 N. Glebe Rd., Ste. 800
Arlington, VA 22201
(703) 247-1500
Web site: www.iihs.org

IIHS is a scientific and educational organization dedicated to reducing the losses—deaths, injuries, and property damage—from crashes on the nation's highways. IIHS's Web site contains research and statistics on drunk driving and information on laws about drunk driving in all fifty states.

International Center for Alcohol Policies (ICAP)
1519 New Hampshire Ave. NW
Washington, DC 20036
(202) 986-1159
Web site: www.icap.org

This nonprofit organization is dedicated to helping reduce the abuse of alcohol worldwide and to promoting understanding of the role of alcohol in society through dialogue and partnerships involving the beverage industry, the public health community, and others interested in alcohol policy. ICAP is supported by eleven major international beverage alcohol companies.

The Marin Institute
24 Belvedere St.

San Rafael, CA 94901
(415) 456-5692
Web site: www.marininstitute.org

The Marin Institute works to reduce alcohol problems by improving the physical and social environment to advance public health and safety. The institute promotes stricter alcohol policies—including higher taxes—in order to reduce alcohol-related problems. It publishes fact sheets and news alerts on alcohol policy, advertising, and other alcohol-related issues.

Mothers Against Drunk Driving (MADD)
511 E. John Carpenter Frwy., No. 700
Irving, TX 75062
(800) 438-6233
fax: (972) 869-2206/07
e-mail: information: info@madd.org
　　　　victim's assistance: victims@madd.org
Web site: www.madd.org

Mothers Against Drunk Driving seeks to act as the voice of victims of drunk driving by speaking on their behalf to communities, businesses, and educational groups and by providing materials for use in medical facilities and health and driver education programs. MADD publishes the biannual *MADDvocate for Victims Magazine* and the newsletter *MADD in Action* as well as a variety of fact sheets, brochures, and other materials on drunk driving.

National Center on Addiction and Substance Abuse (CASA)
633 Third Ave., 19th Floor
New York, NY 10017-6706
(212) 841-5200
Web site: www.casacolumbia.org

CASA is a nonprofit organization affiliated with Columbia University. It works to educate the public about the problems of substance abuse and addiction and evaluate prevention, treatment, and law enforcement programs to address the problem. Its Web site contains reports and op-ed articles on alcohol policy and the alcohol industry.

National Commission Against Drunk Driving (NCADD)
244 E. Fifty-eighth St., 4th Floor
New York, NY 10022
(212) 269-7797
e-mail: national@ncadd.org
Web site: www.ncadd.org

NCADD is a coalition of public and private organizations and others who work together to reduce impaired driving and its tragic consequences. The Web site has a searchable database of abstracts of research studies that makes an excellent research resource.

National Highway Traffic Safety Administration (NHTSA)
1200 New Jersey Ave. SE, West Bldg.
Washington, DC 20590
(888) 327-4236
Web site: www.nhtsa.dot.gov

The NHTSA is an agency within the U.S. Department of Transportation. It is responsible for reducing deaths, injuries, and economic losses resulting from motor vehicle crashes and alcohol-related crashes.

National Institute on Alcoholism and Alcohol Abuse (NIAAA)
5635 Fishers Ln. MSC 9304
Bethesda, MD 20892-9304
Web site: www.niaaa.nih.gov

The National Institute on Alcoholism and Alcohol Abuse is one of the eighteen institutes comprised by the National Institutes of Health. NIAAA provides leadership in the national effort to reduce alcohol-related problems such as drunk driving.

Research Society on Alcoholism (RSA)
7801 N. Lamar Blvd., Ste. D-89
Austin, TX 78752-1038
(512) 454-0022
Web site: www.rsoa.org

The RSA provides a forum for researchers who share common interests in alcoholism. The society's purpose is to promote research on the prevention and treatment of alcoholism. It publishes the journal *Alcoholism: Clinical and Experimental Research* nine times a year.

Responsibility in DUI Laws, Inc. (RIDL)

PO Box 87053
Canton, MI 48188
e-mail: info@ridl.us
Web site: www.ridl.us

RIDL believes current DUI laws are too harsh and are aimed more at criminalizing and punishing responsible drinkers than curbing drunk driving. RIDL's mission is to educate the public and lawmakers about the misdirection of the current laws, take the steps necessary to get the current laws repealed, and to provide alternative suggestions for dealing with the problem of drunk driving.

Secular Organizations for Sobriety (SOS)

4773 Hollywood Blvd.
Hollywood, CA 90027
(323) 666-4295
Web site: www.secularsobriety.org

SOS is a network of groups dedicated to helping individuals achieve and maintain sobriety. The organization believes that alcoholics can best recover by rationally choosing to make sobriety rather than alcohol a priority.

Students Against Destructive Decisions (SADD)

255 Main St., Marlborough, MA 01752
(877) 723-3462
e-mail: info@sadd.org
Web site: www.sadd.org

Originally called Students Against Drunk Driving, SADD's mission later expanded to provide students with the best prevention and intervention tools possible to deal with the issues of underage drinking, other drug use, impaired driving, and other destructive decisions. SADD's

Web site has statistics on teens and drunk driving along with information on how to form local SADD chapters.

Substance Abuse and Mental Health Services Administration (SAMHSA)
National Clearinghouse for Alcohol and Drug Information (NCADI)
PO Box 2345
Rockville, MD 20847-2345
(800) 729-6686
Web site: http://ncadi.samhsa.gov

SAMHSA is a division of the U.S. Department of Health and Human Services that is responsible for improving the lives of those with or at risk for mental illness or substance addiction. Through the NCADI, SAMHSA provides the public with a wide variety of information on alcoholism and other addictions.

For Further Reading

Books

Bjorklund, Dennis A. *Drunk Driving Laws: Rules of the Road When Crossing State Lines.* 2nd ed. Coralville, IA: Praetorian, 2008. Details every drunk driving law for every state, including the District of Columbia. Includes legal limits for intoxication, criminal penalties, driver's license sanctions, fines, and other information.

Gately, Iain. *Drink: A Cultural History of Alcohol.* New York: Gotham, 2009. Covers the history and culture of alcohol, which has been used as both a medicine and a mind-altering product since at least 8000 B.C.

Marczinski, Cecile A., Estee C. Grant, and Vincent J. Grant, eds. *Binge Drinking in Adolescents and College Students.* Hauppauge, NY: Nova Science, 2009. Contains the newest information on binge drinking and how this type of alcohol consumption (drinking to get drunk) differs from social drinking, chronic drinking, and alcoholism.

Martinic, Marjana, and Fiona Measham, eds. *Swimming with Crocodiles: The Culture of Extreme Drinking.* New York: Routledge, 2008. Examines the rapid and heavy drinking behavior by young people in a number of countries. The authors argue that a new term—*extreme drinking*—should be adopted to fully describe this emerging behavior.

Pennock, Pamela E. *Advertising Sin and Sickness: The Politics of Alcohol and Tobacco Marketing, 1950–1990.* DeKalb: Northern Illinois University Press, 2009. Documents three periods of national debate over the regulation of alcohol and tobacco marketing. The author concludes that the politics of alcohol and tobacco advertising reflect profound cultural ambivalence about consumerism, private enterprise, morality, health, scientific authority, and the regulations of commercial speech.

Seaman, Barrett. *Binge: What Your College Student Won't Tell You.* Hoboken, NJ: John Wiley & Sons, 2006. A former *Time* magazine reporter offers a revealing look at life in the dorms at twelve residential colleges. He found college life to be rife with binge drinking and drug abuse, rising suicide rates, casual relationships with students more likely to "hook up" than date, and tensions surrounding race and sexual orientation.

Storm, Jennifer. *Blackout Girl: Growing Up and Drying Out in America.* Center City, MN: Hazelden, 2008. One girl's story of alcohol addiction in her teens and early twenties.

Wechsler, Henry, and Bernice Wuethrich. *Dying to Drink: Confronting Binge Drinking on College Campuses.* New York: Rodale, 2003. Includes devastating anecdotal accounts of tragedy associated with binge drinking on college campuses and offers models for change. Plans are tailored to parents, students, and communities that want to address the problem.

Periodicals

Chavez, Linda. "Redefining the Problem Won't Make It Go Away," *Jewish World Review*, August 22, 2008. www.jewishworldreview.com/cols/chavez082208.php3.

Drug-Free Action Alliance. "Keep the Minimum Legal Drinking Age 21," 2008. www.drugfreeactionalliance.org/documents/21WITHcitations.pdf.

Dyer, Bob. "Sobriety Checkpoints Are Intrusive and Ineffective," *Akron (OH) Beacon Journal*, October 2, 2007. www.ohio.com/news/dyer/10235276.html.

Evans, Bill. "Alcohol Regulation Protects Community," *Salt Lake City (UT) Deseret News*, September 21, 2008. www.deseretnews.com/article/1,5143,700260206,00.html.

Everett (WA) Herald. "DUI Checkpoints: A Line We Shouldn't Cross," January 9, 2008. www.heraldnet.com/article/20080109/OPINION01/377586068.

Heimoff, Steve. "Alcohol Advertising: Is There a Reasonable Solution?" September 29, 2009. www.steveheimoff.com/index.php/2008/09/29/alcohol-advertising-is-there-a-reasonable-solution.

Hicks, Marybeth. "Only Things Plastered Are Walls of House," *Washington Times*, July 1, 2007.

Medical News Today. "Light to Moderate Alcohol Consumption: Exploring the Health and Protective Benefits," November 23, 2008. www.medicalnewstoday.com/articles/130289.php.

Miller, John J. "The Case Against 21," *National Review*, April 19, 2007.

Morris, Sophie. "Cheap Booze Ban Will Not Stop Bingeing," *Independent* (London), November 13, 2008. www.independent. co.uk/opinion/commentators/sophie-morris-cheap-booze-ban-will-not-stop-bingeing-1015519.html.

Mothers Against Drunk Driving. "21 Minimum Drinking Age Effectiveness." www.madd.org/Parents/Parents/Research/View-Research.aspx?research=22.

Nelson, Toben F., and Traci L. Toomey. "Drinking Age of 21 Saves Lives," CNN. com, September 29, 2009. www.cnn.com.

Parker, Robert Nash. "Colleges' Misguided Plan for Drinking," *Los Angeles Times*, August 27, 2008. www.latimes.com/news/print edition/opinion/la-oe-parker27-2008aug27,0,3747225.story.

Rabin, Roni Caryn. "Alcohol's Good for You? Some Scientists Doubt It," *New York Times*, June 15, 2009. www.nytimes.com/ 2009/06/16/health/16alco.html.

Roan, Shari. "Tempest in a Bottle," *Los Angeles Times*, September 1, 2008. http://articles.latimes.com/2008/sep/01/health/he-drinking1.

San Diego City Beat. "Befuddling Booze Ban," November 6, 2007. http://sdcitybeat.com/cms/story/detail/?id=6339.

Sawyer, Freeman. "Drunk Driving Checkpoints Can Save Lives," *San Antonio (TX) Express-News*, December 1, 2008.

Stringham, Edward. "Nothing to Toast in California's Proposed 'Dime a Drink' Tax: False Claims About Alcohol's Costs and Lost Wages Are Being Used to Push Tax Increases," *Reason*, April 20, 2009. http://reason.org/news/show/1007376.html.

Tarm, Michael. "New Ignition Interlock Laws Aim to Reduce Drunk Driving in Six States," *Huffington Post,* January 2, 2009. www.huffingtonpost.com/2009/01/02/new-ignition-lock-laws-ai_n_154795.html.

Taylor, Lawrence. "Technology Alone Won't Tackle Drunk Driving: Ignition Interlock Devices Promoted by MADD Will Do Little to Stop People from Driving While Intoxicated," *BusinessWeek*, November 30, 2006. www.businessweek.com/technology/content/nov2006/tc20061130_489512.htm.

USA Today. "Our View on Legal Drinking Age: Would an Age 18 Minimum Curb Alcohol Abuse?" November 26, 2007. http://blogs.usatoday.com/oped/2007/11/our-view-on-leg.html.

Web Sites

Alcohol Cost Calculator (www.alcoholcostcalculator.org). This easy-to-use tool is designed to help teachers, parents, lawmakers, and children's advocates calculate the toll serious alcohol problems are taking on their communities. A special calculator for kids is available to assess the number of young people in their communities who are likely to have a problem with alcohol.

Checkpoint USA (www.checkpointusa.org). This site opposes roadblocks and checkpoints, arguing that they are obstacles to freedom and the right of Americans to travel freely within their own country.

Don't Serve Teens (www.dontserveteens.gov). This Web site, a collaboration of several government organizations, is part of a national campaign to prevent underage drinking. Students will find the state-by-state legislation section useful for reports.

DUI Blog (www.duiblog.com). This blog is maintained by lawyer Lawrence Taylor, who defends those charged with driving under the influence. He posts about drunk driving laws he considers to be faulty or suspect.

National Conference of State Legislatures (www.ncsl.org/programs/transportation/DrunkDriving.htm). An excellent resource for state drunk driving laws and articles about drunk driving and alcohol-related fatalities.

Why 21 (http://why21.org/). This Web site offers a history of the minimum legal drinking age and also facts and articles in support of a minimum drinking age of twenty-one.

Index

Picture Credits

© ACE STOCK LIMITED/Alamy, 64

AP Images, 34, 45, 49, 54, 59, 72, 80, 88, 94, 105, 111

© epf model/Alamy, 22

© imagegallery/Alamy, 11

© isafa Image Service s.r.o./Alamy, 41

© Dennis MacDonald/Alamy, 75

© Mira/Alamy, 28

© Photofusion Picture Library/Alamy, 14

Justin Sullivan/Getty Images, 99

Steve Zmina, 8, 17, 27, 38, 47, 52, 66, 78, 85, 92, 100, 104